The Secrets of Space and Time

June 10-2013 begun to —
Sept. 4-2013 2nd X

ALSO BY MASSIMO SCALIGERO

The Light (La Luce): An Introduction to Creative Imagination

The Secrets of
Space and Time

by

MASSIMO SCALIGERO

Translated by
ERIC L. BISBOCCI

LINDISFARNE BOOKS
2013

2013

LINDISFARNE BOOKS
An imprint of SteinerBooks / Anthroposophic Press, Inc.
610 Main Street, Great Barrington, MA 01230
www.steinerbooks.org

Book design: William Jens Jensen
Cover image: *The Upper Antelope Slot, Arizona* (Shutterstock.com)

LIBRARY OF CONGRESS CATALOGING-IN-PUBLICATION DATA
Scaligero, Massimo (1906–1980).
[Segreti dello spazio e del tempo. English]
  The secrets of space and time / Massimo Scaligero ; translated by
Eric L. Bisbocci.
    p. cm.
  ISBN: 978-1-58420-130-4 (pbk.) — ISNB: 978-1-58420-131-1
(ebook)
  1. Space and time. I. Title.
  BD632.S3313 2013
  115—dc23

                                                        2012040480

THE SECRETS OF SPACE AND TIME

Who can penetrate space or encounter the stream of time? Only those who are not fooled into believing that freedom from sensory conditions is attainable by moving beyond a space and a time considered real because of their measurability. The reality of time and space is immeasurable. It cannot be attained by overcoming the given forms of measurement, but rather by overcoming measurement itself. For this to occur, we must know how and why measurement arises; we must know what the spirit wants by containing within measurement the substance of its eternal telling of tales, whose truth alone justifies measurement—the transitory vision of what space and time are in their divine forms.

The world is the world that becomes visible to us. By becoming visible, the world remains unknown; it preserves its silence and solitude by way of its appearance. *W*

The world's orgy of loud noises and tumults is the most secure barrier to the secret silence—the vestment of the world's divinity.

Nonetheless, the world hides in order to be discovered; it hides by allowing its spatial-temporal vestment to be gathered. The world is elusive whenever it allows itself to be grasped in terms of space and time—which concern the human being, not the world.

The world continually returns to its secret by allowing us to accept it as it appears, by allowing itself to be the object of dialectics and to be measured. It is as if abstract thought, mathematics, and physics—all of which interpret the world—guard this secret by preventing us from entering into it.

This secret belongs to the thinking that unknowingly conceives the world by sanctifying the world's unreality as truth. It conceives the world by forming space and time out of a *s/t* thinking fabric that it then utilizes to think of them as separate and apart from itself; as necessary; as measurable. A spatial-temporal measurement, however, ceases to be of value to the human being who thinks, dreams, creates, or cognizes the mystery of death.

For such a person, the multiplicity becomes that which has never existed as an autonomous objectivity, that which never seems devoid of its inner continuity and, therefore, conditioned by measurement. For each measurement is contained within it and transcended.

— 2 —

If the world appeared whole and substantial, and not in its vestment of multiplicity, we would not need to establish a direct relationship between entities; we would not feel the urge to conceive spatial and temporal connections. For, within a single point, we would have the whole world.

Space and time are nevertheless helpful to us, for we become aware of how, in conceiving them, we are on the path toward discovering the non-spatial and non-temporal value of things. In conceiving space and time, we *already* dissolve them into an idea without knowing it. We place the sensory things before us into an ideal circle that we have not, as yet, the power to see as such.

Space and time are not conceived to justify the multiplicity but, rather, to restore this multiplicity to its profound syntheses. Woven of space and time, these syntheses are merely reflected by the multiplicity.

In truth, we as thinkers already draw the world out of space and time whenever we employ them to represent the world. All the space we conceive exists within our thinking, as does the whole of time that we measure.

Thus, we do not need to be as large as the space we conceive; nor do we need to live the whole duration of time that we evoke.

– 3 –

As thinkers, we always have the feeling that the true relationship between physical entities exists at a level other than that of the mineral realm where we encounter them. Such entities, encountered at the level of minerality, appear foreign to one another. Their singularity is their reciprocal opposition.

We can have only a *presentiment* of the deepest relationship between entities; we cannot perceive it. Counting tends to take the place of this relationship and, consequently, constitutes the most immediate relationship—that which is visible.

Because we are unable to gather the profound relationship between such entities, counting becomes the preliminary means by which to overcome the reciprocal estrangement of the world's objects. Though it is the correct way to begin moving toward the truth of things, it would certainly be a mistake merely to continue counting.

Mathematics and physics are true as a means by which to identify the world's living element in its negated form. The world that is shattered, broken into many parts, and that takes on the vestment of the shattering can be directly interpreted by mathematics and by physics, but only to the extent that this interpretation is immediate and temporary. Counting is, therefore, the *temporary* form by which the multiplicity can be reunited; it does not constitute the rediscovered unity.

Mathematics and physics are true only with respect to their own level and abstract function. Assumed as the truth, they are erroneous. An object's size and physical phenomenology do not constitute the object, but rather what the object in its essence is *not*.

Even when the art of counting is refined to a form of sublime calculation, it is always the art of primitives who are capable only of *counting* the things before them. Bound to the numerical interpretation of the multiplicity, they fail to arrive at the reality of this multiplicity for they ignore the countless syntheses possible to the thinking independent of numbers.

We move within the extinguished life of things and convert their death into readings by numbering them, by establishing equivalence, by translating physical processes into mathematical terms. As a result, the movement of thought becomes alienated from its own life and creates, out of its death, an outer relationship—logical, mathematical, physicochemical—which can be projected in the form of mechanicalness.

– 4 –

Whereas the machine can *reproduce* movement only abstractly, we human beings are actually *able* to move provided we know how to move, provided we become aware of our movement by possessing it.

The machine's movement exists only as an abstract (thought) relation between its various reciprocally unrelated parts. Through the utilization of their estrangement and opposition to one another, these unrelated parts are nonetheless *compelled* to act in uniformity.

This unified action, under constraint, can imitate movement without itself being movement. The imitation of movement is *A Force* nothing more than the mechanical utilization of a force that does not belong to the machine, which would itself be incapable of functioning without such a force. Neither machines nor those of us who build them possess this force. If we were somehow able to possess it, machines would be unnecessary.

Because movement is exclusively a suprasensory event, we never perceive *what moves* but, rather, *what has been moved*— which, in turn, enables us to deduce movement. When we employ a machine to imitate movement, we inevitably appropriate the forces of the physical world without any knowledge of their real nature, or of the inner aptitude that this requires. We utilize these forces and come to know only their abstract phenomeno-logical laws—not their authentic laws or suprasensory principles.

It is not the world of machines that is immoral but, rather, our relationship to such a world, for we are simply unaware of how this relationship unfolds at the point where we initiate it.

A machine's movement through space is therefore dually deceptive. First, it has no relation to us as cognizing beings. Second, such movement does not belong to the machine itself, whose immobility always lies in the dead materiality of its parts. Rather, it belongs to thought, namely, to thought's life-less relation to space. The machine never moves, nor does any-thing ever move it. Such immobility corresponds to what is lifeless, to what is compelled to simulate the movement that undoubtedly occurs. However, neither the machine nor any human being who *abstractly* thinks about movement actually possesses it.

As an organism, the machine is nonexistent. As a seen object, the machine symbolizes our impotency to enliven directly the dynamic we think about, as is the case when we articulate the image of a gesture in the movement of the arm that carries it out.

It is therefore senseless to try and paint a picture of a machine, for example. If anything, we can produce only a photograph of one. A painter who depicts a machine is either a photographer or a person who knows little about the creative process. To depict a machine is like depicting a mathematical formula, which is precisely what it is. It prohibits penetration of the life lacked by the machine while allowing only for reproduction.

The metaphysics of a machine is nothing more than the psychic secretion of simplistic thinkers.

The machine is *itself* the privation of realized thought. We human beings temporarily need machines inasmuch as we ignore the life that dies out in thinking—the life of the will that moves our corporeal being.

We need machines during this precarious phase of our earthly experience. We can indeed make use of this transitory mediation provided we do not create a fetish out of a tool.

– 5 –

From an absolute point of view, each place in space is as valid as any another; only qualitative distinctions exist.

We think we pass through space simply because we move. In reality, we transport ourselves, namely, the immobility of our trunk and head. Only the non-sensory force, articulated in our limbs, can truly move. We make use of this will force as long as we are unaware of its origin or mode of expression. We merely perceive the effects of movement, but not the moving force that we secretly incite by means of thought.

We move from one point in space to another and mechanically attempt to reunite the two points, to be situated with our consciousness-bearing bodies at the point opposite us. We can reach such a point imaginatively—but not corporeally—through the movement of thought, or through the movement of the will aroused by thought.

But even this does not constitute a passage through space. For the will force alluded to is articulated in the limbs, so that only the mechanical summation of steps can cover a given distance.

Only by experiencing our *own* movement in space can we really claim to pass through space. However, we do not possess this movement; instead, we make use of it only insofar as it is unknown to us. Consciousness can, in fact, express its own being by means of corporeality only insofar as it is present at each point of space through the power of its own movement, a movement that is currently a mere abstraction.

We do not move though space simply because, unlike a color, we do not *see* it. Our movement through space is merely the perception of ourselves at successive spatial points. We pass through the air, just as we pass through water by swimming. We do not, however, pass through the space that we imagine yet fail to perceive. By passing from point to point, we continually establish an imaginative (or thought) relation that symbolizes our movement through space.

But this movement does not belong to us. As long as we fail to relinquish our relation to the sensory realm, no point in space can ever be crossed by walking to another—regardless of the point in question. This is because we are incapable of distinguishing the "qualitative" element from its spatial value. A place is able to exist only because we identify it.

– 6 –

The space we imagine crossing is merely a deduction.

This deduction is relative to a movement carried out by the body, which, as the will's immediate vehicle, is not *itself* responsible for carrying out this movement. Only slightly do we *will* the will that moves such a vehicle in the depths. With respect to the space we deduce, the human body always remains fixed in its physical corporeality; it can be moved only by the transcendent will streaming in the blood and articulated in the limbs.

Though we move, we actually do so by continually keeping still, by staying put within an immobile organism whose true movement does not belong to us. Our true movement (if we observe well) is exclusively the movement of thought.

Only within thinking can we will directly, or truly move. Imagination is already this movement of the will within thinking.

The forces that govern matter within us exist separate and apart from us; we merely perceive their manifestations. Such forces give rise to the movement of our limbs. But to move bodily matter—which is to truly operate in space—is something foreign to us.

We do not move our bodies in the way we *can* move thought, provided we truly think. We perceive bodily movement; we imagine or feel it, but we do not experience its ascension and self-expression in corporeality in the way we can experience the *forming* of our own thought—the only movement we can exclusively claim as our own.

We do not perceive the movement we are in the act of carrying out but, rather, the movement we have already completed. At each point and in each instant, we merely perceive the end product of a movement within which we feel ourselves.

It is the leg movement that we could carry out for miles within a closed circle or along a road from city to city. Only such movement means flowing within the space of those forces that experience space. Such forces continually transcend us regardless of our body's movement from one point of space to another. We merely perceive the body moved by unknown bodily forces. However, for these forces to act, we must encounter them by means of thought. Yet, we are not quite sure of just *how* we encounter them, or of how they act.

This does not constitute our experience of space but, rather, our possibility to deduce space. Because we are incapable of distinguishing the incorporeal image of space from its bodily support, or even the metaphysical realm from its physical counterpart, we think we actually pass through space. It is as if going from place to place had the power of changing our relationship with the materiality of a place. This relationship, however, is unchanging regardless of where we are.

Therefore, it is as if we were always at the same point.

The relation between our point of departure and our point of arrival is merely a relation of thought, which is the only movement that we are currently able to carry out. Not only does thought make the being of space possible, but it also makes the appearance of space—its negation—possible.

– 7 –

Spatial points do not exist. Each point we identify is the exhaustion of space, or the exhaustion of its physical appearance. At each point we can discover our being in space, which is never the case.

At each point we pursue the same mirage: the movement not possessed by us, which nevertheless moves us corporeally. Therefore, when seeing other places, new countries, new beings, we do not discover things by overcoming space; rather, we discover them by conforming to the juxtaposition of objects and places. In so doing, we nourish ourselves with the secret idea of space.

We conform to the juxtaposition of places and of things by retracing their inner continuity through a movement that belongs not to us but to the profound bodily forces articulated in the legs.

We walk by mechanically utilizing the movement of our legs, by conforming to the juxtaposition's abstract relationship. Though we are *subjected* to this relationship at each point we come to, we unconsciously tend to reestablish, by way of each point, a relational unity through a movement that (if we observe well) lacks the power to unify. Only thought has such power. A person asleep, taken from place to place and then back again, is oblivious to what transpires. Only the person who transported the sleeper, or who witnessed his or her arrival or departure, can attest to such movement.

The walk that takes us from place to place springs
from a suprasensory movement that is imperceptible to us.
Nonetheless, we make mechanical use of this movement by
converting it step-by-step. Thought allows us to realize this
physical movement, whose value lies merely in the relation
between points or between moments. In fact, on the basis of
a mere shifting (or changing) of places, our movement can
be substituted by allowing a car to transport us while we are
immobile.

Such movement is still not the spirit's articulation within
corporeality, nor is it us in the *act* of movement. Rather, it is
our need to repeat continually (by means of sensory perception) our relationship to the life forms that, unlike our world
of thoughts, are incapable of simultaneously existing within
us. For this reason, we must be here one moment and there
the next so that thinking can think about and reconnect what
seems opposite it and what, in the opposition, appears separate
and numerous.

– 8 –

The presence of thinking within perception resurrects the multiplicity in unitary forms so that the eye can behold the space
between two horizons as *one*. However, we cannot simultaneously be at every single place that we see and think about, for
we lack the eye's visual simultaneity as well as the synthesizing
simultaneity of thought.

We lack the force that is articulated as our corporeal being, a
force expressed in our gaze and in thought.

For this reason, we must experience each point as separate from the next if our intent is to arrive physically at the place we behold or about which we think.

In order to arrive at a given place, we must walk.

Our inability to possess space compels us to move from one spatial point to another.

Though we continually have the impression of passing through space, we actually remain enclosed (and thus immobile) within the *appearance* of space. We never escape this appearance in order to exist truly within the space we think about, or have as thought. For thought alone is space: the possible initial penetration of space.

– 9 –

Though we think about space and imagine it, we are unable to touch it, see it, or seize it. The measure of a distance or of a volume is not space but, rather, a relation necessary to us as thinking beings.

A measurement is not space. It is, instead, a mere convention abstracted from a given reality, a reality that is *itself* an ideal entity and not the physical substance that fills a particular form.

The volume of a cube is never a measurement but, rather, an inner relation whose reality corresponds to an ideal perception, which we do not know how to have as such. The reality of this inner relation is not its void full of a given substance.

The relation between width, length, and depth is always an inner act. We mistake this inner act for the perception of the object, whose form, in actuality, is one that can be thought.

Though a cross may be made of wood, iron, or marble, its reality is not the wood, iron, or marble that fills its form but, rather, *what rises up as form at the point where matter ceases to exist.*

Form thus rises up as an image at the boundaries of matter when an object's matter is no longer perceived. This image is incorporeal; it is comprised of incorporeal thought, whose incorporeity goes unrecognized. It is non-cognized thinking, alive within perception.

The incorporeal experience of thought still depends too much on the bodily support in order for the image to rise up as an image, in order for the fundamental (or suprasensory) essences to free themselves from the symbols of things. Furthermore, the dependency of the incorporeal experience of thought upon this bodily support impedes the liberation of true (or pure) space from quantitative space. While the forces responsible for the chemical transformations of substances operate from the depths of true space, matter is itself woven by way of these forces; form blossoms as its truth.

– 10 –

We should realize that the chemical processes that engender the manifestation and transformation of matter are supported within their essence by the immaterial powers of substances, namely, by the non-spatial powers that weave the inner space of such substances.

These non-spatial powers expel forms that lack the power to subsist at the level of their cosmic creative process. Though they do not impede those forms from petrifying, such powers leave behind, impressed within those forms, the internal geometries that structure in accordance with the original movement.

For this reason, the mineral world symbolizes the spirit, but the fallen spirit—the petrified form that has yet to be re-elaborated. This form is projected as the substance that crystallizes the original form—separate and apart from the spirit and, yet, radically founded on it.

In chemical processes, the spirit of substances is not only present as the power to restore the original movement, but it is also invested with the power of expulsion. This spirit continually breaks the limit of the expulsion that has become materiality. In doing so, it reaffirms the power of expulsion regarding the higher relation it bears into the world. This higher relation enables all substances bordering the sensory realm to be connected as *one*.

What enters space and time is this extra-spatial and extra-temporal relation that persists through distortions in the various combinations of substances.

For this reason, matter by itself does not exist. Matter can exist only if thought—which considers itself the counterpart of matter—is real. Matter exists only if it is supported by the force that thought has a presentiment of, and already actualizes within this presentiment.

The art of penetrating matter is the art of penetrating the perception that enables us to begin grasping matter. It is a question of coming to rest within the spatial-temporal process of perception, that is, of *thought* continually coming to rest within perception. To perceive is to make contact with the life that hides behind the screen of minerality—a life to which minerality owes its existence. In being *something* for perception, matter is already penetrated. Nevertheless, we must be aware of penetrating it.

We need to rest. We need to contemplate. We need to do *slowly* what we always do in haste. We need to rest within the act of seeing and within the act of hearing.

Because space is thought to be physical, matter is mistakenly seen as isolated; we lack knowledge of how to contemplate such matter.

The chemical analysis of matter cannot reach the boundaries of matter if it considers matter to be founded upon itself. Such matter becomes our sphere of imprisonment; its measurable and finite aspect takes on the immeasurable vastness of the thinking that investigates it, thus becoming a mood or myth.

The impossibility of reaching the limits of matter is an impossibility related to thought, to thought conditioned by the limits that enable it to begin seeing matter.

– II –

Matter that materialists take into consideration is an inferior faith. Such matter is merely dreamed up when analyzed without a recognition of the forces that continually become manifest in chemical processes, forces that hold matter in its state of fortuitous inertia.

Whoever views the material aspect of things as reality effectively lacks the ability to understand just *how* we consider things to be real. And, by continually having of the world what can live in our inner being, we believe all things around us to be real except the forces within us that render them so.

Human illness is being unaware of what we actually do whenever we transform our perceiving into an inner activity. Therefore, matter cannot be real in an isolated state from which our perceiving has already removed it. This perceiving becomes manifest only to what possesses it, namely, to a subject without which perception itself would not exist.

Insofar as they depend upon the perceiving to which they give form, matter and space (as physical values) are thought structures inevitably unaware of the movement from which they arise.

For them, the true content of perception is lost.

Although we measure matter as well as space, we do not actually perceive them.

— 12 —

Nevertheless, we think we can master space by moving from place to place while inevitably always bearing the same limit. Scientific knowledge and mathematical logic reassure us of this, as they both create a new metaphysics out of the impotency to cognize the limit. We consider it quite an accomplishment to overcome given distances with greater speed, namely, by reinforcing the illusion that space is conquerable and that earthly limits can be overcome via machines, which are themselves the typical expression of our subjection to such limits.

These limits can be overcome only where they are grasped and cognized. For the only extraterrestrial space toward which we can journey is that which requires the use of a carefully encapsulated missile in which all necessary conditions for our earthly existence are reproduced. And even so, Earth is, in effect, never left behind. This is also the case with the nervous system, whose life can exist only upon the Earth's surface and whose mediation gives rise to the formation of nature's abstract laws. The validity of such laws diminishes as we gradually distance ourselves from Earth.

To become distant from Earth is to *experience* what can be gathered beyond the mediation of this nervous system. But this would effectively be to realize thought's autonomy from intellectualism, to realize an independence from sensory conditions that enables our inner being to explore other worlds and to perceive the life unknown to us on Earth.

Earth is still unknown to those who presumably probe the cosmos. The life that gives rise on Earth to the existence of plants, animals, and human beings is a mystery to them. The mystery that they seek "spatially" is merely the life on Earth that arrives from the extraterrestrial cosmos, a cosmos that cannot be reached unless we know how to encounter it in its various earthly forms.

– 13 –

We think that by moving to other points of the earthly multiplicity—points which, essentially, in purely spatial terms, always constitute the same point—we accomplish something beyond the possibility of having our inner action be independent of where we happen to be, even if such action relates to what this place is worth outside its being a mere place.

A place, in fact, exists only if we arrive or come to a stop there, if we live there. We give it value as an endpoint of a given distance, or as a necessary place of residence. The spirit frees such a place from materiality so that it is no longer part of the abstract multiplicity, any more so than our arrival there constitutes a value beyond the relationship that the spirit establishes with it.

The spirit that does not have to travel or to overcome distances has no need of numerations or measurements in order to comprehend within its unity what, as a disseminated multiplicity, the movement from point to point requires in order for the unitary relation to become reality.

This sensory reality, however, continually deceives us when it comes to crossing or overcoming space, which our spiritual being in turn can actualize through its simultaneous presence at each point of the multiplicity. For the spirit can *be* the spirit only by containing the entire multiplicity within itself.

The joy of moving in space is our presentiment of directly realizing the spirit, which is itself on the verge of actualizing, at each point, what it already super-sensibly possesses. The spirit is on the verge of actualizing, as conscious life, its suprasensory presence within the sensory realm. This suprasensory presence is the world's truth—a truth always contradicted each time we perceive the multiplicity or harbor the illusion that a movement other than thought can reunify this multiplicity. For movement in space is thought itself.

– 14 –

The crossing of space can be only the movement of *what* moves the body. It cannot be the movement of the body—which is moved. Only after the body has been moved can one know of its movement. The same is true of thought, whose movement we can cognize only insofar as it has already been thought.

The movement of thought cannot be cognized before it is thought.

The movement into which a thought is translated is always thought that can be experienced only by becoming an image (or sensation) of the completed movement. Yet, we do not experience an image of the force that enables thought, through its hidden dynamic within the bodily depths, to become the life of this movement.

– 15 –

Only by employing forces that do not need to overcome the sensory limits of space can we pass through what we think of as space. For such forces weave space as a fabric of the world's light.

Space is truly suprasensory; yet only by penetrating its formative weft can we experience this suprasensory realm in the physical world.

We cannot experience space unless we genuinely perceive the sensory realm. Because each perception is imbued with thought, we can draw the initial thought of the being of space from various points of our sense-based perception of Earth. But we do not know *how* to experience thought as an innate movement in which the forces of space already surface.

We do not know how to experience the thought of space— namely, space without a locus but nevertheless concrete—by cognizing a movement that ranges freely insofar as it is free of space. This is the movement of thought that conceives space by crossing it, for there lies, within this movement, the force of space as well as the possibility of actualizing its virtue beyond the sensory limits where true space exists.

The concreteness of those entities considered real is their power of space—a power that only thought can penetrate by acknowledging it as a form of its own movement.

Because we fail to cognize the *thinking* that we employ to think about space, we are oblivious to the possibility of entering space. Consequently, we think that space is overcome only by moving from point to point within the sphere of multiplicity—the sphere from which the image of space rises up to us.

This space however is merely imagined; it can be crossed only by cognizing the formative weft of imagination.

Because we are unaware of how to experience the thinking used to think about space, we inadvertently place this thinking in the outer background, with which we then identify it. We see space as physical and unknowingly place the image of space all around us.

We should feel included in this image of space; yet, we do *not* simply because we are incapable of perceiving space.

Physical space does not actually exist: only the physical (or negative) dimension of space exists.

The modern rationalist who considers space to be a physical entity by identifying it with one of its three dimensions (without noticing the immateriality of the other two) is no less primitive than a physiologist of today engaged in clinically experimenting with thought in the functioning brain of another person.

Though science presumably proceeds by way of precise intuitive and logical processes, it still lacks the logic by which to notice where its effective research trespasses into superstition. This is particularly true when it thinks that space can be mathematically grasped, or when it insists that the universe is penetrable by means of measurements—even though the life of a blade of grass rising up from a clod of earth remains an impenetrable mystery to it—or when it daydreams about moving onto other worlds via machines that, in themselves, symbolize the lack of real movement. These other worlds are perceived, conceived, and interpreted through the mediation of a neuro-sensory structure that is capable of living only at a certain level of the Earth's area.

– 16 –

Therefore, we go from place to place on foot, or by machine; we even fly. However, with respect to a mechanized vehicle, we cannot objectively say that, as travelers, we cover any given distance. Instead, we remain fixed within the machine which, devoid of life and real movement, does not carry out the journey from point to point any more or any less (insofar as the physical overcoming of distance is concerned) than a tossed stone or a projectile—both of which, equally devoid of intent, do not presume to pass through space.

It makes no difference to the machine where it is; spatial value means nothing to it.

From this we can see that a distance thus traveled—which we call conquering space, even to the point of conceiving "spatial enterprises"—is identical to that of a machine incapable of thought, inert and immobile at each point like the arrow of Zeno d'Elea. For the relation between points is only a relation of thought.

This relation, indispensable to those incapable of passing through space, would of course be totally unnecessary if we could indeed pass through space. Whenever we move from place to place we do not experience space; rather, we acknowledge its absence. The absence of space requires an abstract relation.

Because we unknowingly exist separate and apart from the space we have lost, we lack the ability to experience this abstract relation where it is actually carried out. Therefore, our movement from place to place is important to us as something that within itself has the value of movement. This is particularly true with respect to those entities unable to communicate with one another.

This movement (or dynamic) always escapes us; the most we can do is think about it. Though we arouse this dynamic, we do not actually move it. If we could directly move it, we would move the Earth.

This however can never be done from outside by mechanically operating on things that remain things, objects, or shall we say, unmoved matter considered real in its dead abstractness. We would, instead, need to operate from the center of life, which enables things to exist. This is true movement.

With regard to such movement, our own movement is nothing more than a projection into exterior space, into the image of true space—a projection that barely rises up again in the form of abstract thought.

This is because we think only *about* the force that moves our limbs; we do not possess it.

– 17 –

Although true movement can undoubtedly be realized in the physical world, it is a mere sketch of thought's penetration into space. In becoming movement, such thought is imperceptible as the life of movement. In fact, it ceases to remain thought, becoming instead activation in the *depths* of the very force that it is in the *heights*. Both heights and depths are not cognized by our thinking consciousness. They constitute the power of life of thinking, which consciousness excludes in order to become waking consciousness, or self-consciousness.

When stirred up by thought, this imperceptible life is actualized in movement, for it is the non-dialectical force of thought. Until thought realizes its own movement and becomes one with it by freeing itself from the bodily support, this non-dialectical force must withdraw from rationality in order to manifest as a force. It must do so while keeping intact the consciousness developed through bodily mediation. Perception will then be able to penetrate inner space.

Today's physiologists daydream by believing they can experimentally pursue the thinking process in the "functioning brain" of another person. Instead, they always find themselves face to face with their own perception, a perception integrated by their own thinking. No single perception can be thought by anyone other than the perceiving subject. Therefore, the perception we attribute to someone else is really our own—no one else's.

Though a researcher may even trace the physiological processes that accompany thought in the functioning brain of another individual, such processes will always be the researcher's own perception and will consequently fail to evoke any thought other than his or her own.

In truth, the relationship between the cerebral process and thought does not take place outside subjective consciousness. What remains outside and is subject to objective experimentation by a refined physiological study of the brain has nothing to do with thought.

An actual experience of this kind is effectuated only by a deeper thinking, attainable by anyone who proceeds according to the laws of thinking—laws that do not constitute logic. We can follow our thinking by abstracting from our own intellectualism. This constitutes the art of thinking, the art of understanding the relationship between thought and the nervous system.

Just as a mirror has nothing to do with the image that it reflects, so too has the cerebral process nothing to do with the activity of thinking. We can discover this by experiencing the workings of thought.

In truth, each time a physiological cerebral process takes hold of thinking—diverting it from its own autonomy and rhythm—it breaks down the life of consciousness, which in turn can express itself in various gradations: from obtuse, primitive realism—clothed by scientific dialectics—to madness.

– 18 –

Though we think we move about in space, what *actually* moves in space is only our incorporeal being. Our corporeal being is always moved. Similarly, our clothes (or footwear) cannot presume to move on their own while we walk; they are moved.

In reality, it is as if we were always motionless at the same place. For when we arrive at a given point, we fail to realize its communion with the other points already encountered along our path. Instead, we tend to overcome *outwardly* only the non-communicability that, between such points, generates abstract consciousness.

Our presence at a given point exists only in accordance with the corporeal being that excludes all identity and stands as an object between objects, in opposition to them; we can imagine only this corporeal being's spatial relation to such objects.

Because this relation does not change the moment we change places, it is as if we were always at the same point, as if we recognized the place we happen to be—which, of course, is a result of actually being there—as a reference point to other places. Consequently, the places where others stay and establish their points of reference are distant quarters from where we are.

In reality, no place is absolute as a center from which we can move toward others. Yet, each place *is* absolute as the point in which we can exhaust the physical representation of space. This is, in turn, our initial possibility to perceive space, that is, real space—*not* the space comprised of points foreign to one another that, consequently, require connections of outer movement and time. Real space is, instead, the space woven out of the union of all points.

Insofar as being able directly to realize movement within corporeality, there is no space that we can truly move in, for such movement is presently foreign to us and perceptible only by way of its sensory effects. We are essentially immobilized within a relationship to outer physical appearance. Such a relationship confirms the alterity (or otherness) of this outer appearance as the continuous identity of each point opposite us. It does so by virtue of a correlation between points that apparently stands in opposition to us, but, which, if we observe, is nonetheless our own.

And, so, we think we move. But it is as if we were always motionless at the same point, at the same place, at the same "here"—unable to cognize what connects one place to another, regardless of their dissimilarities, unable to cognize what unites such places beyond their reciprocal juxtaposition.

By conceiving space and by feeling ourselves advance in time, we employ this reciprocal juxtaposition to begin uniting these places.

We could come to know the whole of space within a single point. We could begin to perceive, within a point, the space that we imagine if only we succeed in understanding why our physical being has to move from place to place in space. Such places themselves do not constitute space.

Space is the *incorporeity* that makes possible the juxtaposition of bodies.

Bodies have the initial incorporeal relation in space.

All physical points of space are identical with respect to this incorporeal relation, which is a relation of thought. A body that

moves from point to point does not overcome the lack of relation between such points. For corporeality itself constitutes the
juxtaposition that only thought can overcome.

Only the image-idea can overcome this juxtaposition, for
it enables the powers that weave true space to surface within
human perception as the light of the world's being.

We do not perceive space physically. Only by perceiving
thought can we perceive space.

Only the person who actually perceives space can move in it.

In reality, we exist separate and apart from space. Suffering
arises out of our separation from the space that we can only
conceive or imagine.

– 19 –

And, yet, we go from place to place and call this moving. In reality,
we merely assist our own movement, which does not imply perceiving it in the *act* but only as a manifestation, fact, or product.
This perception is so simultaneous with the motor act that we
have the illusion of perceiving this act, or of acting by means of the
motor nerves, which—as one who does not abstractly draw from
Spiritual Science can experience—are nothing more than sensory
nerves. These nerves transmit neither will nor thought; they perceive the already made, but not the process of coming into being.

Perception of the act, of the movement, of the flow of life, or
of the formative etheric forces can be only an inner perception.
By schooling ourselves to perceive our own immediate being, or
its initial immediate movement (thought), we are on the path
toward acquiring this inner perception.

Thought tends to reconstitute unity. In fact, in its initial abstract movement, thought already *is* reunification. It begins by numbering things and establishing conceptual relationships while always proceeding more and more toward syntheses that correspond to the world's truth. The thinking that employs its own movement to arouse bodily movement and see it through to the end lacks the power to manifest *itself* directly as bodily movement. At present, it lacks the power to realize its highest inner aspect, except by way of artistic, cultural, or scientific mediation. Such thinking is still abstract; its movement is lifeless. It is unaware of its own power to operate as a force of space— certainly not of physical space.

When going from place to place, we do not employ the movement of thought—our most immediate movement. Rather, we proceed by means of a non-cognized will force, which is the non-cognized but profound force of thought.

We go from place to place; we overcome the distance that separates us from those we love. We suffer from homesickness. We yearn for the place we have left behind, or for the space that enables us to discover what is connected to the heart. The contradiction inherent in the abstract vision of space is that the unity of all beings and things in the sensory world, possessed by a heart intact, is continually lost. Such unity in the sensory world is fragmented into various places or times, each of which demands to be transcended by the soul.

The pain of being far away reflects our incapacity to actualize, within the world, the heart's communion with the world's entities—a communion that the heart already inwardly possesses.

For the secret of the heart is to keep the weft of space in a non-fragmented state, in a state not fragmented into multiplicity. Wherever space is truly unified, or perceived, an accord of the heart is reawakened.

If space does indeed have a center, it is the human heart. The hope of discovering the secret continuity of things (which in its immediacy is space) surfaces continually from the heart. This is particularly true when our eyes contemplate the vastness of an earthly landscape or of the sky, or when, at the conclusion of a trip, we have the sensation of overcoming the juxtaposition of places.

Each time the magic of a gaze or the magic of thought leads us to exhaust the separation of things in space and in time, we unknowingly live for instants in the heart's accord.

– 20 –

Thanks to memory, we are always at a place that becomes our reference point to the space we freely move in. We remember: we trace back to the heart. All the space we imagine or re-evoke— in the house where we live, on the peak that we climb, on the island upon which we disembark, in the vehicle that we travel in—is always related to our present space. All images of other spaces ultimately lead to the place where we are so as to connect with this place as an image. For such a place does not truly exist physically if we can have an image of space.

Regardless of where we happen to be, we are unknowingly at the center of space.

We must continually identify a place as a point in opposition to space—separate and apart from other points—simply because we are unable to simultaneously be at all of them. We lack the simultaneity appropriate to the gaze that embraces a landscape, or to the thinking that grasps syntheses of thoughts.

We must proceed from point to point; we must overcome the distance between trees along an avenue, all of which lie instantaneously before us.

We are unable to actualize, by means of our bodily presence, the simultaneity available to us in perception and in instantaneous thinking. One by one, we must continually experience the points that symbolize a given distance; sequence consequently replaces the simultaneity temporarily lost.

Because this temporality extends indefinitely, the loss of simultaneity becomes lasting. Simultaneity passes into imperceptibility.

The persistent loss of simultaneity is time.

But it is lost time; simultaneity precipitated.

Each instant is, in fact, a past instant. Duration is not experienced in this way; it is true insofar as it goes unnoticed. No one feels time passing by. Only the hands of a clock, the setting sun, the unfolding flower, are signs of the time that passes. However, they are only spatial signs—the measures of time.

Each instant is a past instant, a fleeting moment that can never be halted without ceasing to be what it is; without ceasing to be a sign of nonexistent (or lost) time, of measurable time.

Beyond its instantaneousness, an instant is time that can be discovered; it is time that can be perceived, but not measured.

In fact, instantaneousness is punctual simultaneity: the possibility of simultaneity that is punctually lost. Each time simultaneity is lost, it becomes time—measurable time.

Exteriorized instantaneousness, in fact, cannot help but identify with the physical future. It is time, but time that never exists—the duration of its flight.

Time, either lost or not experienced in its objective simultaneity, is perception's abstract identity with the sensory processes, which demand that their becoming be projected into the human inner depths. They demand that simultaneity be removed.

The continuity of this removal is time.

But it is abstract time. Genuine time is, instead, the perceived continuity—continuous instantaneousness.

It is space, immeasurable space.

— 21 —

Time is the future that comes to meet us as well as the past that lies within us. Future and past are fused within a present that surfaces instantaneously but is imperceptible in its *continuous presence,* which is simultaneity—identical being, identical flowing. It is simultaneous continuity, continuously lost.

Simultaneity—seen spatially as a symbol and contemplated as a luminous synthesis of thoughts—is the stream of the being that we cannot grasp in its metaphysical unity. For the connection to the multiplicity, by immobilizing vision, interrupts its flow. Thus, we establish an abstract relation between points, or between moments, which are themselves signs of that interruption. This spatial-temporal relation confirms the immobility of our view of the multiplicity: the paralysis of its flow.

By continually requiring perception in order to become manifest, immobility, as a fixed symbol of simultaneity, is imperceptible simultaneity stripped of itself: simultaneity continually broken off into moments by perception.

We are unaware of *how* to grasp these moments as moments, as points of the emergence of simultaneity, or eternity, whose form is simultaneousness. Such moments are annihilated in sensory perception. As part of the finite world, they are simultaneously possessed as small openings beyond the finite realm, and then lost. For this reason, they necessarily always involve an *interval*.

The interval, abstractly overcome and abstractly filled, is time, but lost time—the continuance of its loss.

– 22 –

We can cognize this interval, which is never cognized, by grasping the inner movement that unites one thought to another.

In fact, abstract thinking in need of a quantitative measure (or succession) loses time.

Time exists separate and apart from quantity. Only the specter of time can be measured; time, itself, is immeasurable. Time is not the succession; it is what guides the succession.

Measurable time is finite time; it never exists. It is the past that does not exist. As a non-reality, the past conditions the present, which is nonexistent, as well, since it always passes in expectation of a future that escapes determinability. Time is therefore the present—always awaited and always past. Time is true only insofar as it is lost.

This loss, as continuity, is time that can be intuited. The interval, as a flow, can be perceived by the thinking that grasps its own flow as a synthesis or as simultaneity.

We can discover time wherever it is lost. We can cognize our illusive memory and behold the past that has never really passed. We can discover the spirit's memory, which is real time.

This can all be attained through contemplation, which enables the discontinuity of the finite world to be overcome and the perspective of time to be restored within the simultaneity of thought.

Not only can the spirit actualize memory after death by freeing itself from bodily conditions or during life by virtue of spiritual practice, but it can also actualize memory in rare moments where one has a brush with death. In such a case, the vital (or etheric) body frees itself from the physical sheath for split seconds, only to appear as a synthesis of life's events—an instantaneous panorama of time that surfaces from outside time.

This is true space, which we can experience.

– 23 –

Succession does not constitute time but, rather, time's fall into the enchantment of space.

In fact, the multiplicity correlated to abstract consciousness gives rise to the physical realm of space where our movement (or stay at a place) is merely a physical attempt to overcome the lack of relation between objects. This lack of relation, unrecognized in its non-entity, is incidentally overcome at its own level (assumed as real) by means of an abstract relationship that, in turn, depends on the single elements of the non-relation between objects. Such an abstract relationship requires that objects follow one another, so that there is a "first" and an "after": succession. Fortuity thus becomes order, or nature—time.

– 24 –

What comes "first," or what comes "after," makes no difference to a stone, which could not care less whether one beholds
it now or within a year. Such a relation concerns only human
perception and, consequently, human cognition—namely, our
presence in time.

A novel lies printed in a book, forgotten in a library. By now,
its story has returned to the timeless state in which it was once
born as a product of the spirit. The timelessness of its physical
vestment corresponds to this timeless state. Such a novel is a
timeless object (as are all objects that go unperceived) until a
reader frees it from its solitary state by withdrawing it from the
library and reentering it into time not only as a mere object but
by reading it—by again placing in time the story narrated there.
The story's revivification in thoughts and images is a succession
of events requiring time, determinable time.

Such time is measurable; it does not correspond to the profound reality of things but, rather, to the specter of this reality,
namely, to its incidental form, which we need as a means to
discover time of a deeper reality.

In fact, this specter, contemplated like materialized space,
can lead us to its living being, to its fabric of light.

– 25 –

We must witness the various transformations of a tree's life—
from a cast seed to its initial bursting forth out of the earth, to
its process of growth, flowering, and bearing of fruit. We must

reunite various moments or spatial-temporal images, namely, the various successive aspects of the spatial-temporal specter, or the various sections of the same entity, in order to arrive at the image-synthesis of what already exists entirely within the seed and in each moment of its development.

The secret of each worldly entity is that it appears as a veil by concealing its entire past as well as its entire future—both present and interwoven—which can rise from the veil only by means of imagining-thinking.

Each entity can be intuited as a timeless density of time, as a spatial form of time, in which its own being is already truly complete. Only an entity's earthly appearance must be divided into points and into moments for human perception. The importance of such points and moments lies in their correlation: the resolution of the succession.

Pain within the human soul corresponds of necessity to this illusory relation from point to point, from moment to moment. Such is the pain of the soul, confined to the death of its own space, to the anticipation of its revivification in time—the pain of having to experience itself reflected by corporeal being. By reflecting the soul, our corporeal being sections off its timeless life into a succession of time. As a result, the soul thinks it ages and dies.

Such pain will not be extinguished by measurable time but, rather, by a series of returns to the spiritual time experienced during sleep. Though we will come to know this spiritual time at death, only by drawing from the profound calm that enables the physical, disenchanted dimension to pass over into a timeless weft, can we cognize it in our waking state.

– 26 –

To be bound to perceptive punctuality is to lose the continuity from point to point; it is to lose inner perception. The spatial-temporal *process* of perception is projected into consciousness. From this, the need arises for a temporal succession of world events (both inner and outer) and of movements that connect one place to another in imagined space.

Succession needs the passing time, which in turn always leaves behind a void to subsequent time. Succession is, therefore, the prolongation of time's annihilation—the lifeless image of the original continuity.

It is the protraction of time's nonexistence, for which we cannot help but measure the passing of time abstractly through the use of sense-bound signs.

True time never passes. It is *itself* the passing, which always exists as eternity's rhythmic movement within temporal cycles. It is simultaneity coming into being, a simultaneity that can be grasped only in sections, that is, in moments, or spatial-temporal points that defy fixation—one moment always extinguishing itself for the next.

The magical help that we can receive from time is ordinarily ignored for it arrives from outside time and inserts itself within our inner human form, which is itself woven out of time. It is the miracle of everyday life that is realized within time, which, by passing, is nonexistent. Nonetheless, such time is continually elevated from transitoriness to true time—namely, time comprised of light, time that edifies our spiritual memory.

What we continually free into moments of light from the obscurities of pain, or by virtue of cognition over time, we will one day have as a synthesis (or density) of time.

No illuminating moment is ever lost. Instead, it continually becomes part of a suprasensory form, which in turn cannot become a complete structure unless we work at it over time. This suprasensory form divides up our task into years, months, days, hours, and moments.

This is the ultimate sense of measurable (or nonexistent) time.

Actually, not a single moment of measurable time is ever lost. Each moment is connected to the next according to transcendental affinities that are themselves determined by the profound human will that surfaces within time—in thinking and in ordinary feeling.

We are what we will in the depths. But we do not will the spirit—our free being—there. Instead, we push it away, believing we are free. For this reason, the spirit—namely, the true human being's will from outside time—works within us over time.

Time enables us to divide into years, months, days, hours, and moments, what we would never be able to actualize as the spirit's super-temporality on the physical Earth. This super-temporality presses forth within us as a continuity of events in successions, as well as the synthesizing power of moods and thoughts that succeed each other in time.

This succession conditions the spirit, which, as immediate consciousness, would like to instantaneously rectify error, eliminate evil, overcome distances, and actualize love on Earth—all of which, however, require a series of movements in space and time. They require patience, namely, the emergence of that force which alone has the capacity to develop while obliged to confront its own shattering—a reflectivity that has become reality. This force is the force of waiting, the virtue of discovering itself at the point where, fragmented and atomized by the support, it is led to think of its death as life within lifeless space and lifeless time, both of which are sanctified by abstract thought and quantitative science. Such a force can defeat darkness only by experiencing and cognizing its own negated power of light.

Earthly darkness is really the death of that light which has become reality, a reality that enables the phantom of space and the specter of time to operate.

Nonetheless, patience and waiting lead willing individuals—even for fleeting moments—to the limits of measurable time where the spirit can be perceived. In order to operate in earthly nature, this spirit assumes the darkness of multiplicity—the measurable vestment of space and of time—as its very form.

– 27 –

True time never passes; it is *itself* the passing that manifests as the symbol of an entity graspable only by means of the sensory signs that fix its flow. But, in reality, this entity is lost wherever we believe its flow to be fixed.

Time is what we can continually feel being lost or never seized. Not only is it impossible to contemplate time as one would a place somewhere in space, but also it cannot be fixed like space, whose reality is to be outside time—for objects know neither a "before" nor an "after." Meanwhile, the unreality of space lies in its value as sensory space, for objects know neither an "in front of" nor a "behind," neither a right nor a left.

Time is the space that we never penetrate yet unknowingly yearn. It is space perceivable as a suprasensory weft. Such time, however, is immeasurable.

Measurable time is lost time. Philosophers who take its punctual becoming into consideration declare such time to exist by not existing and not to exist by existing. In its abstractness, it is measurable time whose existence lies precisely in its relation to a given moment—a moment that exists only as a sentiment aroused by the thinking bound to measurability.

It is time projected onto a past that we re-evoke or onto a future that we imagine, whose each and every determination is nevertheless fixed in relation to other moments for the sake of its necessary passing. Such moments can themselves be determined as signs of what we never possess: each moment being the cancellation of all the others.

Continuity is really the secret cancellation of each moment carried out in the depths by our inner life. Because this inner life fails to perceive itself, it lives in moments that are continually lost and not in the continuity that it unconsciously actualizes within itself through the passing of such moments.

Felt or thought about, time is real only insofar as it goes unperceived. We unknowingly actualize time within ourselves precisely to the degree that we refrain from fixing it. In so doing, we continually lose time and, yet, give it meaning exclusively for what it is with respect to its measurability.

Because we are oblivious to the continuity that can be realized through our disengagement from measurable moments of time, we inevitably lose time. We are unaware of becoming free because we do not know *how* time truly helps us by flowing unseen.

For this reason, we conceive infinite time as an abstract eternity, imagined as a succession of time extending indefinitely—an eternal time awaited and lost. It is punctually lost, for never is a moment of it consciously freed from its transitory state. As a result, we are always in anticipation of the following moment.

Meanwhile, time does not pass. A fleeing instant is nonexistent simply because it cannot be determined. Never has an instant fled for never has one truly been perceived.

– 28 –

Aside from its quantitative measurement, the passing of time is really a human feeling. It is either the pain of the good and the beautiful that we go about losing, or the joy of the good and the beautiful that we possess (or await). But the good and the beautiful that we can draw from the past, from the passing of time, or from our anticipation of the future, are essentially the good and the beautiful that we can elevate from measurable time to the height of pure ideas. In so doing, we transport ourselves (if ever so briefly) into true time.

This is possible because imagined time is woven out of time itself. Therefore, philosophers who still knew how to think have affirmed that time does not exist by existing, and that it exists by not existing. By limiting themselves to a speculative vision conditioned by the very limit that they had come to see, these philosophers translated into concepts the perceived non-determinability of time as well as the manifesting of its continuity. They were able to accomplish this without entering the secret of time.

The secret of time is essentially the secret of that thinking which thinks time, renders our memory of the past current and projects the future before itself. Such thinking condenses time by becoming activated in the depths and discovering itself as pure movement.

This more intense thinking does not draw from spatial-temporal determinations, which it must continually connect and overcome; rather, it draws from its inner force, which is free of determinations. This inner force can overcome spatial-temporal determinations through its independence of them. Thought must *acquire* this independence—which is not freely given to it—regardless of its independence in the incorporeal world from which it springs. Only the bodily support (or nature) freely gives itself to thought, which in turn draws abstract time and abstract space from it. By conceiving them as entities separate and apart from it, or in opposition to it, thought never experiences abstract time and space. Instead, it loses them.

Meanwhile, true space and true time do not exist separate and apart from thought. They are the fabric out of which the soul clothes itself in order to make its appearance in the world. The soul does not see this fabric simply because it fails to perceive itself. It thinks it sees by virtue of the physical eyes, whereas it *itself* has the power to see by means of our bodily eyes. Therefore, thought assumes that the time and space within it come to meet it from outside, for it sees them outside as a spectral projection of *that* which it does not know how to gather as an essence; it sees them as a measurable spectrality.

This spectral projection is the unseen movement of thought that penetrates the earthly realm after submitting to its conditions.

The spirit that fails to penetrate earthliness, by perceiving it in opposition to itself, experiences its spatial-temporality.

This earthliness, kept in its alterity by the spirit, comes to meet us. It is clothed in space and time, which we are incapable of gathering within ourselves as a fabric of light.

Such a specter is the weft of lost light that we can discover by contemplating the world, provided we gather those forces that stream in us during contemplation.

It is the world's spatial-temporal light—a light identical to the light by which the soul clothes itself in order to become articulated in corporeality and thereby connect itself to the world.

– 29 –

Each specter is a light temporarily lost—a light that simultaneously dies out and rises again in the earth's colors. The dying out of the light enables the human eye to see. We behold the world and think we see light. In reality, we see mere objects clothed in the dying light. The dying out of the light fragments the light into colors, which is the light's refraction.

The light that we fail to perceive in its suprasensory unity— or illuminating power—is the light that we know as fallen, divided and reflected. Only the practitioner can see light in its wholeness, invisibly bursting forth before becoming fragmented and refracted, before being transformed into electromagnetic, thermal or particle radiations.

Warmth, like light, is really suprasensory. It is the light's power of movement that operates as the secret structure of entities and as the bodies' cohesive force. In its essence, this warmth is the warmth of love; it is the light's life that creates or rises anew—as celestial fire or as earthly fire. As above, so below.

Within color (as within the form of those entities that we behold) lies the hope that matter will again become light—the light that it *is* in the depths; moreover, there lies the hope that matter will reawaken as the light of ideas, as the warmth of life within the human soul.

This is the Earth's secret. It is the secret of the light's rebirth insofar as it rises up as the fabric of thought, within thought, by ceasing to die out into the specter of space, or into the specter of time.

We can reascend from the specter to the light.

Immediate thinking is the light of life that encounters the fallen forms of universal thought within the world. The principle of those fallen forms is this non-refracted, whole light.

Just as forms and colors are already the light that barely rises up from death, or from its encounter with earthly darkness, so, too, is true light the light of immediate thinking within perception that enables the eye to see. This light is quickly extinguished because it fails to cognize its own enkindling.

The sun's light is cosmic light prior to space and time. It extinguishes itself by becoming sense-bound on Earth and by allowing itself to be seized in spatial-temporal processes. Consequently, it becomes warmth and the colored vestment of things. This light's encounter with darkness gives us the image of light, but not the light itself.

This image nevertheless rises up as thought. Light is the fabric that enables thought to have form.

Non-refracted, whole light is the very fabric of the non-reflected, non-abstract thought within us. This fabric of non-reflected thought can encounter the light within the world's colors by reascending from the spatial-temporal process of sensation to its pure time, to its space of light, or light of space.

– 30 –

The tree that we contemplate at a given moment is only an image-symbol of its entire history, of its non-refracted body of light. As an image-symbol, it is already the refraction in time and in space that enables form to appear.

In the spatial present, we can gather the tree's temporal being as unified and restored light. This is not an event in time that can be summed up in the form of a chronicle or science. Rather, it is a being woven of time, or the completeness of time—an inner form that contains its own past, present, and future as a single weft.

This inner form appears in that image; it hides and reveals itself as a refracted moment of light. No dialectical formula has the capacity to grasp this inner form, for its language—the soul's movement—is immediate. It is the archetypal light that we are unable to gather in its intact radiance. We are used to pursuing the juxtaposed projections of its earthly negation because we see them as real forms of space and time.

Each entity in space refers to its own light form as well as to a time structure imperceptible to the senses. This light form and

time structure are of the same luminous fabric of the imagining
that imagines this entity in time and places it in space.

– 31 –

The imagining that imagines space and the passing of time needs
time to unfold from one thought (or representation) to another.
Each concept, or image, is compelled to follow the other by
means of its dialectical process. Such a process is conditioned
by sensory vision and, consequently, by the single points and
moments in need of being related, or else by their occasionally
necessary relationships.

Nonetheless, those who propose to speak about an event,
a theme, or a book they truly understand for the purpose of
helping others grasp it in its entirety, will experience a moment
in which the whole event, or theme, appears within a single
thought (or image). The entire content is simultaneously present within this single synthesis-idea, which one cannot truly
say enters time. Rather, the whole of time is contained within
it, instantaneously, until it unfolds in a dialectical process that
requires time—namely, time that passes.

This synthesis-idea is truth. By unfolding, it becomes lost so
that other thinkers, capable of truth, can newly reconstitute it
in its timeless reality. Within its fabric, this synthesis-idea is a
density of time that manifests as a flashing perception of time—
of time that does not pass but is, instead, a complete continuity.
Simultaneously interwoven within it are all the thoughts that, in
their singularity, insist on following one another by unfolding,
one by one, in time—in the passing of measurable time.

They unfold in lost time.

Such time always disappears unobserved into suprasensory time, that is, into time's real being—the hidden continuity. We can contemplate this hidden continuity by perceiving the essence of thinking within ourselves, which is not the thinking that connects points of space or moments of time to one another. Rather, it is the relationship itself actualized. Such a relationship already exists as a synthesis: as the world's essence.

Certainly, this relationship does not precede thought, for it can surface only as thought's living fabric—namely, as the world's innermost thinking.

– 32 –

Space is certainly not the thought of space, nor the idea of space. Yet, only by *experiencing* the fabric of such thought, or by *perceiving* the idea of space, can we encounter space.

Thought is what we unknowingly have of space. Because we fail to experience space *as* idea, it becomes a mere idea to us.

The idea (namely, each movement of the idea) enables us to be at the threshold of true space.

Nonetheless, thinking enters outer time by ordinarily conforming to lifeless space, as well as to the physical sphere whose discontinuity is temporarily overcome by means of the relation between points. This lowest form of time (outer time) enables thinking to maintain its rhythm.

Timeless in itself, thinking must exist within time so as to overcome fortuitously the discontinuity of space. Thinking binds to time, which is represented by means of its space-bound movement.

Measurable (or lost) time is essential to sequence of events, or thoughts, just as it is to a discourse that is spoken, written or even read. The reality of such a discourse is always a synthesis that thinking actualizes, separate and apart from time, by withdrawing the real (non-discursive) meaning from the discursive sequence.

Thinking can actualize this synthesis by discovering continuity, a continuity whose very fabric is the simultaneity proper to living thinking. As the power of willing, this living thinking is the principle of motion in space.

– 33 –

Thinking, modeled according to the world's measurability, loses the simultaneity from which it is drawn; it accepts the spatial juxtaposition of things and their temporal succession as real. But this temporary vestment of reality is *itself* the movement of thought that encounters things and establishes a rational order between them.

Unless thought recognizes its own spectrality and draws from its original being, this rational order will be able to grasp only the mere shadow (or specter) of the being of space and time. Only in this way can thought avoid being conditioned by its own reflection of the multiplicity.

The spiritual discipline of thinking is the art of perceiving Earth's real fabric, the living space of entities. The nuclear energy that we presently arouse on the physical plane (without an awareness of its internal process) is only an indirect manifestation of this living space.

The spiritual discipline of thinking is the art of entering the world's secret. Earthly limits cannot be overcome by physically investigating more and more objects. Rather, we must eliminate the limit within the thinking engaged in such an investigation, a thinking whose degree of penetration is unchanging whether directed toward the cosmos or toward an atom.

This earthly limit is actually an inner limit that cannot be overcome within objects themselves. Beyond this limit lies the possibility of moving in true space, in the space that we are unaware of thinking. We lack the power to imagine this space outside its sensory reference. Such thinking—its vital weft cognized—is the same inner space that surfaces within the soul by tending to express its extraterrestrial rhythm within thought. For such thinking (as pure space) is universal time.

Today, however, those set on transforming our loss of rhythm into a systematic and mechanical order continually oppose this extraterrestrial rhythm. By means of forces withdrawn from the universal order, the existence of this extraterrestrial rhythm resonates against the order of nature, which in turn reacts.

Today, this rhythm must not be sought outside for it is inseparable from thought—the element in which it directly flows.

– 34 –

Because of their determinateness and measurability, abstract space and time devoid of life have nothing to do with Earth's being—the living (or invisible) Earth. Instead, they have everything to do with Earth's dead aspect. Life is invisible; only its manifestations can be seen. While a true ascetic may have beheld—and still behold—life, it can certainly not be said that a mere scientist has ever glimpsed it.

What we consider real with regards to Earth is what has ceased to exist, namely, Earth's debris or dead exteriority, which we dignify and translate into science and technology. This debris or dead exteriority clothes itself in thought in order to be of value.

In truth, we think by means of what is dead of the Earth. But the thinking that draws structures from such death is alive in its inner weft. Its life is not cognized but continually dies out as dialectics.

The life of this thinking—capable of discovering itself in luminous syntheses on this side of its lifeless spatial-temporal forms—is identical to the life that weaves living being. For the life of thinking possesses the principle of this living being within itself. Though true Earth is invisible, we can work toward its advent through the redemption of thought or through pain.

Earth's reality is identical to that of a seed whose physical weft dies in order to open up to new life. The earthly weft that dies is the sense-bound reality of present-day human beings and culture; whereas the new life that consequently arises is the non-cognized movement of thinking that we nevertheless employ to think of the sensory world as reality. Herein lies the contradiction.

The light of a future cosmos presses forth within Earth's dying shell, which is the earth, measurable in terms of space and time. Though this earth is abstract, we sanctify it as living without consciously experiencing even the slightest thread of its life.

By means of the new germinal forces of thought, science legitimizes this decrepit and unraveling sheath, while culture idealizes it.

Such is the dialectics employed by materialists and spiritualists of all stripes. They are capable of thinking about matter, energy, the atom, the spirit, or metaphysics by means of a thinking that contains the very foundation that they seek via such thinking.

This foundation must be discovered by at least a small number of individuals. Each path toward the spirit that fails to lead to the recognition of this foundation becomes an error. For each path toward the spirit cannot help but appeal to such a foundation, to its life—even if its intent is to affirm what ignores life.

Whether in regard to matter or metaphysics, cybernetics or Zen, neo-positivism or Yoga, our present-day thinking is imprinted by Earth's corpse. Its life is the life that is continually lost as thought, grasped by Earth's dead forms. For this reason, we believe in the reality of matter while weaving tales about the spirit, or while concerning ourselves with oriental ascetical theologies, or *even* while making judgments on the vanity of appearance.

Although we negate matter, we are unaware of just how real we consider it to be and how radically attached to it we are. Above all, we do not even have the slightest notion of just *how* we consider matter to be real. We fail to notice that we continually engage matter in a game of relationships that, even as spatial distances, are nonetheless relationships of thought. These thought relationships have to do with matter that undoubtedly exists (i.e., a rock, a house, a suit, a torrent, or the body of a tree, animal, or human being) but whose very foundation is *not* matter. Otherwise, matter would be the world's essence, which it is not, simply because, as matter, it is always moved (or united) by something else.

Because we have yet to acquire the organ by which to *perceive* what moves (or unites) matter, we can only think about it, and do so unknowingly.

Matter is moved (or united) by what we unknowingly imagine. This is because imagination simultaneously regards the imagined as both real and unreal. Physical objects are considered real, but not that which allows them to rise up as a reality within consciousness. Each object is endowed with a physicality that (upon closer observation) becomes real only insofar as it is permeated by thought. In fact, an object's dimensions are themselves nothing more than thought itself. Nothing of an object passes into consciousness except the object's clothing of itself in the forces of consciousness.

This is true even of the Earth upon which we walk, or of the apple that we take hold of and bite into in order to taste. Such is the objectivity of the world, an objectivity that the senses mediate by virtue of thought. This objectivity would exist very little in its physical and outer alterity, if it did not continually refer to an essence (or principle) that certainly cannot be the abstract law of nature, much less matter.

Such matter never moves anything. Instead, it is always moved.

− 35 −

Thus, the deifiers of matter (materialists, positivists, or scientists on the cutting-edge) who think that consciousness can be explained by way of physiological processes ignore the manner in which matter is considered real. They avoid acknowledging the objectivity of the forces that enable them to consider the world objective.

They think that such forces are the product of a presumed physical reality, which itself would *not* be real in the absence of such forces. Because it is sanctified by thought, physical reality is considered real. But this physical reality is mere superstition that stands in opposition to thought as a product estranged from it. Thought itself considers it as such.

It is superstition to think that matter lies at the heart of the world and not notice that it is *thereby* construed as an essence. In truth, matter is an *idea* that we do not know how to recognize as such.

We unknowingly conceive an ideal worldly principle and call it matter.

This is like an idolater incapable of distinguishing the idea of God from the fetish that he or she worships as God.

− 36 −

Matter nevertheless exists, as do objects and entities clothed in matter. Yet, if we observe well, this matter can exist only because it stands in opposition; because it is something other; because it is outside. We are not inside matter, which, insofar as it rises up as a limit to our being, is *itself* responsible for our separation from it.

What truly penetrates and moves matter (i.e., a tree's edifying force) cannot have abstract matter—which itself requires thought, measurement, or a relation of space and time—outside it, or in opposition to it.

When we see matter, we have no choice but to struggle against it from outside simply because we are unable to truly penetrate it. Unlike the edifying force of a tree, we do not permeate matter. Though such a force is present and working within us, organizing our corporeal being and moving our muscles, it is foreign to us. We do not cognize it.

Because we are unable to possess the matter that constitutes our bodies, we are compelled to see matter outside us, that is, a world whose positive aspect consists of a series of spatial-temporal processes in which perception, permeated by thought, finds expression. But this perception leaves the world impenetrable by drawing only representation and sensation from it—namely, that which leaves the world behind in its appearance, as if this were its objectivity.

Meanwhile, this objectivity recedes into itself, deepens, and becomes a perceptible identity if only we discover *that* of the spirit which is already active within the appearing of this objectivity. This appearing is to be discovered for, within it, the being of the world and that of the spirit already meet: the world discovers the human spirit.

Those who observe this appearing can witness how the spirit already encounters the world; they can thereby discover an identity that is already actualized. If unrecognized, this identity itself becomes the limit of objectivity—the shell. It is not seen as the spirit's form but, rather, as the form of something else.

For this reason, matter seems to hide its secret within itself; it appears outside us. Meanwhile, matter is not outside us insofar as perception is identity.

This identity goes unnoticed. What merely seems to reveal itself is halted the moment it appears; thus halted, it appears as alterity.

In reality, perception is still devoid of conscious light. We do not actually see nor contemplate what we look at. Rather, we always look at it fleetingly, for all too often we are satisfied only with its immediate appearance.

To contemplate is to recognize the identity, to discover the synthesis of thought and perception that already exists. Perception, therefore, can exist as only an inner resonance.

Each perception is already, within itself, a living thinking in need of recognition, a living thinking that we need to open up to.

— 37 —

We exist separate and apart from matter. We are subjected to it. We are forced to see matter outside us. Nonetheless, we can feel that we are within the thinking that thinks about matter. We can realize that the soul (or thought) does not actualize the forces that permeate matter within the body.

We can understand why it is that we must die.

In reality, we must see that what stands in opposition to us exists only insofar as it is ruled by those inner forces we fail to possess.

Even when matter exists in a state of non-organic unity, it belongs to the play of these forces, which we continually think about but fail to perceive. Matter, assumed as a reality founded upon itself or separate from such forces, is not only the self-contradiction of thought, but also an imprint of death projected upon the whole of culture. It gives rise to the anguish of individual souls.

The outer matter that we consider reality is real only with respect to those forces that permeate it by way of relationships that vary from the mineral to the human state, according to a manifestation that we are able to concretely perceive and clearly think about. Though we consider such forces and relationships real, our inability to possess the thinking that thinks about them precludes us from encountering their reality.

We are subjected to matter as if it were a reality opposed to us, a reality apparently self-founded. For, within thinking, we do not actualize the spirit that really governs matter by organizing it until such matter expresses itself in our corporeal being as form.

We must come to see that what stands in opposition to us exists only insofar as it is governed by the spirit. Nonetheless, the spirit that eludes us in objective matter is engaged in supporting and forming matter. It streams to us as thought at the point in corporeality where it is no longer engaged in such a task. Such thought, however, fails to actualize the spirit.

If thought actualized the spirit, we would not have dead matter in opposition to us—matter conceived in its dead state and codified as such. Such matter always transcends us; we endure it until death, the moment of revelation. Instead, we would experience matter as life, from within. We would rule over matter, which currently rules over us even though we have the illusion of dominating it scientifically or mechanically. We would penetrate matter by way of the spirit and, thereby, perceive space-time. We would possess the movement of our limbs—a movement we normally arouse without possessing.

Our incapacity to take hold of matter in its concreteness and to take on its reality is replaced by an abstract activity that tends to overcome spatial and temporal separations and juxtapositions by means of measurements that represent the sole truth of present-day science. It does so by utilizing various forms of mediation such as machines and physical instruments of investigation whose very structure limits them to the measurable realm, to the unreality of matter—namely, to its death.

– 38 –

Outer matter that we consider real, exists; it is there regardless of whether we call it concrete, imaginary or essentially energy. If this matter is merely reduced to further conceptualization and not to the demands of an inner act, it is impossible to resolve; it is impossible to penetrate by means of a concept, or even by means of what we ourselves might say.

Such matter cannot be ignored for it exists. Matter cannot be resolved by means of theories or experiments that invariably confirm its alterity by assuming this alterity to be real, independently of the cognition that experiences it. Therefore, we need to reckon with matter in some other way.

Conceptually audacious, nuclear physics does not grant us a single step beyond the ordinary relationship between thought and perception. The alterity's limit is not in the least affected. Though matter is rendered useless in the form of elementary particles, anti-particles, "strange" particles and so on, it always ends up as something other, as something impenetrable.

Nowadays, the perception within which we encounter the physical world requires that we be truly conscious of the forces that express the physical world in the form of images and sensations. New scientific paths open up to the researcher capable of observing the current of life that flows within perception. This life current is always halted by alterity, by the alterity accepted as an image and converted into thought.

The researcher's task is to dwell within perception so as to gather the inner forces that already encounter the world. Ordinary perception is a continuous evasion from the inner content of perceptions.

The thinking that penetrates perception can notice how it already unknowingly begins penetrating matter in ordinary perception.

What thinking fails to penetrate remains outside; it remains outside together with what goes unnoticed, though penetrated. By remaining outside, it is the alterity that comes to meet us as something other in order to be further penetrated. It is matter that appears to be self-founded.

Matter nevertheless exists insofar as it is directly perceived in its initial opposition, in its initial occurrence: insofar as it is perceived as fortuitously being something other, which is already an unconscious identity. This unconscious identity suffices for the appearance of matter as well as for non-cognized perception, which always perceives by eliminating the subject of perception.

For this reason, measurable space and measurable time inevitably arise as measures of what the "I" does not know how to penetrate, and of what, consequently, manifests in opposition to it.

In fact, the "I" does not directly perceive the world's objects. Rather, it always has them reflected by bodily consciousness; it has them by means of the sense organs' spatial-temporal processes, which coincide with those of the world. But within these spatial-temporal processes, life appears as the non-spatial, non-temporal content of perceptions. The incapacity of the "I" to receive this content within these perceptions leaves worldly matter outside it. Such matter objectively manifests as a sign (or symbol) of the "I's" lack of penetration into the perceiving consciousness—a consciousness that is overly identified with corporeal being, with the spatial-temporal mediation of perception.

– 39 –

Perception, whose nucleus of light dies out into sensation or representation, is continually lost. Such perception leaves matter outside itself. We are unable to allow the profound identity—for which the sense world and the spirit world are the unequivocal life—to resound inwardly. Consciousness paralyzes this identity; matter is exteriorized.

Matter never really exists alone. The spirit always governs matter outside our thinking consciousness, which in turn clothes matter with appearance.

As minerality, matter is nothingness, but nothingness insofar as it is virtually the "void" that conceals the spirit. The fullness of matter therefore constitutes the spirit's power of negation. This nothingness is not the nothingness normally expressed in terms of weight and measure; it is, instead, the void where transparent thinking can be actualized.

Contemplation of the mineral world conceals the sense of Earth's mystery, as well as the mystery of life that can overcome earthly weight. Such contemplation, however, must draw from the void of forms used by the spirit to edify life.

We err whenever we equate matter with fullness. Such matter is never truly perceived in the immaterial state to which it owes its existence. This immateriality enables matter to aggregate and be perceived.

Such matter must be supported by matter, which in turn must lean on other matter, and so on—until, logically, the support can itself no longer be matter.

This explains why matter weighs; it is simply unable to have inner support.

Only the forces that overcome gravity have inner support. They overcome gravity by drawing the plant up from the earth, or by streaming in the blood and in the movement of our limbs. These imperceptible forces weave the inner space—or time—of entities. Unlike the egoic consciousness that enables alterity to rise up, these forces do not have matter opposite them and, therefore, do not leave matter outside them.

These imperceptible forces permeate matter; they remove its weight, leading it back to another value that is, itself, imperceptible. Only by possessing the immaterial presence of these inner forces can we perceive such a value. Sensory processes certainly do not enable us to perceive it and, even less so, do physical instruments.

— 40 —

Matter weighs. It does not support itself; instead, it is always supported.

But matter can be supported only by what does not need support and does not weigh.

What weighs is not true in itself, insofar as it weighs; for its weight is not a sign of its being, but of its non-being.

Weight is the sign of death.

If we observe well, everything that is measurable, weighs. The energy vibrations that can be physically measured refer to something corporeal and are, consequently, subject to weight.

If what supports a weight also needs support, then it, too, weighs. Consequently, it cannot help *but* lean on something else until, finally, it leans on what can really support it, that is, on what is itself not subject to weight.

Ultimately, matter can be supported only by what is *not* matter. It must lean on what is weightless in order to lean on what truly supports it—namely, on what does not need support.

Whenever we explain weight by means of gravitation, we naively employ laws to account for phenomena—laws that are their abstract transcription.

Furthermore, the simple objection that all earthly matter is held together by the centripetal equilibrium of a spherical body, moved by universal forces of attraction and repulsion, confirms—for those who fail to understand how matter founded upon itself lacks a sense of reality—matter's dependence on immaterial forces. Such forces rule the gravity that enables each physical body to weigh.

– 41 –

Only a force devoid of weight can inwardly move a weight-bearing body. Such a force does not cognize weighing. It penetrates matter and moves matter because it can possess it. Matter does not weigh on it.

The force that moves matter does not experience its weight. Such weight is instead experienced by what must exert effort to move matter mechanically or to move it from outside.

Only human beings who bear within their corporeality the very forces that (in their capacity to overcome gravity) do not experience weight can feel an object's weight. We lack these forces. Although we call upon them to act, we do not possess them. We therefore experience weight; we must exert effort to lift a weight.

Only human beings incapable of mastering the force that annihilates weight within the human organism experience an object's weight. For this reason, weight continues to symbolize the insufficiency (or limit) of our earthly power.

What comes to meet us from outside as something weighable and measurable symbolizes our impotence to possess the life of our corporeal being: the life that lifts matter—the Earth's spirit—from the depths.

Earth as matter therefore escapes us; it weighs. Only at death do we cease to experience its weight, or does it cease to weigh at all.

Only the human being experiences weight. An object that weighs does not experience weight—nor does the force of gravity or the power that can overcome gravity.

We experience weight whenever we give *only* physical support to it, whenever we translate the force capable of annihilating the weight within us into muscular exertion so as to support such weight, or to lift, or to move from the outside.

Therefore, the forces that build up the human body do not experience bodily weight, which is, instead, experienced by the "I." Because of its limitation to bodily consciousness, the "I" draws a sense of itself from the bodily support. Such bodily consciousness can recognize only the existence of outer bodily matter that weighs.

This bodily matter, the spirit's initial (or primitive) experience of the physical world, depends on the function of the muscles and the important role they play. Though these muscles themselves do not constitute the *force*, they are created by the force that does not know how to manifest directly in the physical world, as it does in the muscle's corporeal structure.

The only force capable of overcoming the body's inner gravitational force is that which builds and moves our muscles. Unable to overcome such a force independently, these muscles are themselves a sign of the force's limit; they mediate the force's abstract manifestation.

Apart from this force, each motion is the mechanical imitation of movement—a sign of our incapacity to move ourselves (or anything else) in space.

Everything is a weight in need of support, including the human body.

– 42 –

It is therefore an illusion to think that we can mechanically overcome the force of gravity. No machine can overcome the force of gravity insofar as it is inextricably bound to its sphere. Because it is not subject to weight, the force of gravity (which does not have matter outside it) is *itself* the cause of weight.

The machine weighs by nature. In fact, it cannot do anything but weigh because its function corresponds to the utilization of its inertia, namely, to the use of the purely mechanical relationships of its idle parts. Though these idle parts are themselves devoid of any reciprocal relation, they are compelled to act as if they indeed possessed such a relation.

The machine is nothing outside the sphere of earthly gravity. Extraterrestrial spaces are incapable of receiving the machine simply because it is devoid of reality outside the earthly sphere— or outside the gravitational influence that envelops Earth up to a given altitude.

A machine's structure is such that it can establish spatial relations only where space is abstractly related to the physical points that we perceive, and not to non-earthly places whose materiality (as the facts will show) is a projection of our way of perceiving here on Earth.

A machine cannot overcome gravity for the simple fact that it expresses gravity; it translates gravity into figures (or readings). *A machine enables us to utilize the force of gravity so as to create not what is overcome but rather what (by continuing to draw toward Earth) can imitate the motion of the force that draws toward the heavens.* We are deluded into thinking that we can lift ourselves toward the heavens, or that we can penetrate cosmic spaces. Such acts merely represent our continuous attempts at abstract measurement while we remain motionless and enclosed within a sphere, and more than ever within the earthly limit.

Such a weight continually needs support; it does not leave Earth.

– 43 –

We measure weight, but not the weighing that arrives from the immeasurable realm.

We measure the effects of weighing but fail to perceive what is expressed as weight.

We experience weight, or heaviness, and we know that something weighs; we know that a force draws objects down toward Earth's center. Therefore, we speak of gravitational attraction. But, in effect, we lack thinking capable of penetrating this perception. We do not really know what to make of an object's descending movement, namely, its compulsion to fall when dropped from above.

Nonetheless, if we carefully observe, we see that the falling of an object is never a movement but, rather, the object's tendency to exist without movement—inert. An object falls until making its immobility felt.

Weight impedes movement; it stands in opposition to what moves the world. Weight is matter's opposition to the power that once unified it and left it behind.

In order to manifest as movement, the force that moves the world has need of what weighs and stands in opposition to it.

The forces that build up the plant need the earth to manifest their formative power.

In reality, weight is what must be lifted. Movement cannot exist without weight because the force that moves the world would have nothing to move, nothing to lift again toward the heavens.

Deprived of internal movement and abandoned by the power that first unified it, matter—in need of itself—tends to unite with other matter. It tends to form a single body with that which it is ultimately supported in order to realize its own immobility and thus stand—according to its own privation—in opposition to the creative forces. By forming a single body, it is also able to stand before the immaterial power of the creative forces' petrifying will, in accordance with this will. Herein lies the meaning of weight.

The lack of a foundation constitutes weight; it constitutes the need of a foundation as well as the creation of an opposition to this foundation, born of such a need.

Pain and cognition enable us to free ourselves from the illusion that matter is founded upon itself. In different forms, they are the emancipation of the soul's immaterial life from the resonation of what weighs.

The soul's immaterial life, however, needs death in order to free itself from this resonation. By liberating the immaterial life of the soul from the weight of the body—deemed heavy only by a consciousness bound to corporeal being—death introduces this life to what is truly incorporeal.

Matter is in fact dead. Only individuals unable to see that matter is true only in reference to its own foundation elevate it to the value of life.

Matter, uprooted from its foundation, symbolizes death; its value can be translated only into mathematical expressions. This matter, whose very existence necessitates the presence of space and time, is the one recognized by current science and present-day culture.

And so, in order for what is graspable—insofar as it weighs—to be considered real, we must be able to perceive spatially as well as temporally.

By regarding matter as real, we attribute a foundation to it that, upon closer observation, is recognizable as the foundation of thought.

– 44 –

We think by means of what is dead, by means of what is true for the spirit only insofar as it is part of the death process. We continually draw the forms of our mental picturing and thinking from the Earth's dead vestment. Within these forms, the living force of thinking presses forth without being cognized—as does the life within a seed once its sheath dies in the Earth's womb.

Forces of death must stimulate this thinking in order for it to actualize its own life. Though matter seems to stand in opposition to the spirit, the appearance of matter already constitutes the spirit's encounter with the death forces of matter. It confirms the rebirth of thought life. Such life became extinguished when the spiritual realm (no longer retainable by human beings) was consigned to dialectics, to texts, to oral or written transmission—a surrogate of direct transmission or of what could no longer be transmitted, but only lit up, within the free human being.

Having lost the life of thought, we have come to our *present* form of thinking, which no longer depends on revelation or tradition. This loss has resulted in our perception of a lifeless, material universe: the multiplicity in movement (appearance) that lends itself only to measurement.

Measurement is a sign that the world's reality has become lost. Yet, it also marks the beginning of our possibility to enter the world by recognizing, in calculation, the *outline* of a movement of thought in what is real. This outline can be brought to fulfillment if, at a given moment, we are able to abandon calculation altogether, which serves only as an introduction to true investigation.

While appearance itself is measurable, that which appears is not. Instead, it is always thought or imagined but never recognized as thought or imagination, since it is identified with appearance. Thus, each spatial and temporal relationship, whose inner tendency is to restore the inner form—namely, that which, by appearing, is not the appearing itself—is necessarily arrested at the point of its abstract measurability.

If we intend to find the reality or *living form* of things, we must abstract from what is measurable. Though the measurable realm, science, and physical investigation can help us discover this reality (or living form), we must nevertheless free ourselves from them by cognizing their limit and entering into what they tend to shut out. Moreover, we must perceive the force they oppose, a force that affords them the possibility of such an opposition.

The third (or physical) dimension is really opposite the spiritual dimension. It can be recognized as a volume's power of projection negated within the physical limit by the spatial-temporal processes that seemingly fill it. Today, the human being is unable to gather the power of projection from outside, namely, from outside the limit. In ancient times, true architectural edification was actually the wisdom (or art) of the limit's conformity to the structuring power of space—insofar as it could be perceived.

The third dimension conceals the secret of "form," which enables thought to rise up and find its freedom.

If we wish to encounter space, we must set aside all physical points of reference. This will enable us to gather the *relationships* between such reference points—relationships that consist of length, width, depth, not to mention the very connections between these relationships. If we wish to encounter time, we must imagine a tree devoid of all physical appearance, so that we can follow, by means of contemplation, the movement of the formative force that contains its past, present, and future.

By discovering that we always possess nothing more than the *form* of the physical world's appearance, we are on the verge of again finding the *reality* of existent matter, or the reality of objects and entities clothed in matter. As we have seen, such form exists only as an idea.

This idea—that we fail to grasp as such—is identified with the world's spatial-temporal processes.

– 45 –

All in all, if I want to know what a block of marble is beyond its weight, measure and physical-chemical properties, I must ultimately realize the impossibility of uncovering its innermost being by digging inside the marble itself. For, by doing so, I will merely encounter more marble and new measurable relationships, in new form—which are effectively nothing more than ideal relationships.

What spontaneously arises within me, however, is the naive feeling that in order to have the essence of this marble, I would need to search within—a gesture reflectively the inverse of what makes the intuitive penetration of an object possible. Each ideal penetration of an object is a profound penetration into oneself.

This gesture is opposite to that used to search matter for the purpose of experiencing an atom or elementary particle. Such an atom (or particle) is effectively experienced, but without any knowledge of its real spatial-temporal position and with the obvious illusion of having reached the boundaries of matter.

Meanwhile, the opposite is true if we think that beyond such boundaries we can encounter the extra-material world of formative forces.

Similarly, we would not think of entering a mirror in order to find a reflected object; nor would we think of studying the mirror's surface in order to understand how the mirror can be entered.

The so-called "atom" is not the point where matter begins to form, but its opposite. It is the point where matter, having already been formed, disintegrates; it is the point in opposition to that of the formative forces—even if it is governed by these forces or, better yet, disintegrates by virtue of their radical presence.

– 46 –

We can discover the spirit where matter rises up: not where it ends, or disintegrates. At the point of disintegration, the inverse direction can effectively be encountered only by means of the spiritual current that governs it. Otherwise, this inverse direction would not merely govern a specific scientific experimentation, but the culture connected to it as well.

The current of the formative force of space that enables spiritual space to pass over to a three-dimensional world expresses itself, in both the first and second dimensions, by means of its own rhythmic force. It becomes a volumetric projection at the point in which it affirms itself as the order of minerality (or third dimension) by encountering and imprinting the lower earthly forces.

By way of the mineral multiplicity, the most powerful dimension manifests as physical spatiality.

In reality, we must discover the third dimension. Clothed in materiality, this third dimension is the requisite for perceiving and for thinking.

The mineral dimension conceals the force of a powerful but lost dimension that makes possible the formation of present-day human thought. By thinking about dead matter, such thought begins to geometrize space and to see time proportionately, for the projective power of the third dimension lies deep within it.

The architecture of space belongs to the third dimension, a dimension born of the spirit whose power it carries into minerality. The architecture of space does not belong to the dimension that rises up out of the mental realm as an abstraction by way of its physical appearance. This would be the intellectualization of its inverse direction: the ahrimanic imprint of thought. Thought must free itself of this ahrimanic imprint if it is to actualize the power of the third dimension: or its power of movement.

The movement of which space is woven becomes thought's perception of itself.

In truth, thought formed within the mineral dimension has the power to reweave the inner spatial structure of minerality if it can grasp only its own movement.

Thought can even allow itself to be devoted to nuclear research—which is the inverse of such a movement—as long as it is aware of what it does.

Thought is truly the initial form of penetration into matter. Ideal perception is the first conscious movement of the force that governs matter within the body.

We tend to become conscious of this force whenever it expresses itself as thought. For this reason, it initially appears in a reflected and abstract form. Yet, only insofar as it escapes consciousness can this force within the body effectively govern matter, particularly with respect to the processes of growth. Thought will one day realize such a force within itself.

This force edifies life by penetrating matter, by moving it within its essence, by engaging it in the rhythm of the worlds. One thing is the calcium found in nature; another is the calcium circulating within in the human organism, enlivened only to support the energies of a thinking person.

– 47 –

The immobility (or inertia) of the mineral world conceals the secret of our earthly presence.

Clothed in a mineral sheath, we human beings experience *immobility* in order to cognize, in its objectivity, the *movement* of the forces before us. The impossibility of truly moving in space and perceiving the continuity of time enables us to think about space and time. It allows us to conceive the spirit's creative movement.

Our immobile, earthly being enables us to cognize the spirit's movement.

If we were not founded on corporeal minerality and thus confined to the substantive immobility of the physical structure, we would not be able to experience sound, light, or even the living forms that express the spirit's movement on Earth. If we moved in synchronicity with the spirit, we would not be able to cognize its movement.

In order to perceive the spirit's movement, we need to make use of our immobility, which, at first, inevitably appears as the ego's power. We then need to direct this egoic power by lifting it from a corporeal reality to a spiritual one. In so doing, the egoic power formed within our earthly corporeal being becomes the suprasensory power of the "I."

Gradually, we will begin to realize the immobility that lies before the movement of thought. This will, in turn, become the *capacity* of immobility that lies before the flow of feeling, before the streaming of the will—the immobility that lies before the stirring of instincts and passions.

In truth, we err by identifying with thought, with an abstract thought devoid of life. To be able to perceive thought in its movement while remaining immobile is to connect with it in the depths, where such movement is the light of life. This is the secret of our future spiritual practice.

– 48 –

The spirit that justifies the human form must govern the mineral, plant, and animal nature within us so as to express itself by means of this nature. The spirit's action is the continuous struggle against nature so that life can be the *life* of the spirit.

A deeper movement of the spirit in nature—the only true movement—continually requires that we be overwhelmed by instincts; it requires that we fall prey to illness and death.

We barely begin to possess this movement within thinking.

Within the thinking that thinks about matter, we barely begin to actualize, as an abstract movement, the spirit's permeation of matter—a permeation that supports physical life.

We find before us, devoid of spirit, matter that is permeated by the spirit. For only by setting aside the spirit's life element can our thinking be actualized outside the spirit's direct relationship to the bodily organism.

Thinking can cognize life only insofar as it begins to oppose it; and so, it gathers only the appearance of life. This appearance, uprooted from what appears—that is, from what it clothes—is unreal and abstract; it is measurable.

Only what is dead can be measured.

Nonetheless, what is dead and measurable becomes experience by rising up as thought. Though the possibility of life exists within death, we ignore this possibility whenever we cognize only the objects of thought, not thought itself.

We do not really think in order to draw from the thinking that thinks the experience, namely, from the logic that has yet to be cognized.

The latest phase of logic is actually a sign that the original thinking called forth by logical necessity is lost. Symbolic logic is the thinking that we render useless, the thinking continually evoked in relation to predetermined forms.

Such thinking no longer arranges the measurable realm. Rather, it is *arranged* in accordance with the measurable realm, which the dialectics of death today genuinely needs in all cultural fields.

Thinking, modeled according to three-dimensional space, creates its own limits and renders them dialectical in order to form, out of fictitious space, a logical kingdom for itself.

– 49 –

Dimensions arise as our attempt to reconstitute the space from which we have been expelled.

The space from which we have been expelled is Eden, the original spiritual earth—lost paradise.

We employ thinking to draw abstractly and unknowingly the etheric and spiritual dimensions out of the physical (or third) dimension, which conceals the *negated* inner depths. We do so without noticing that only one dimension belongs to the sensory world; the other two dimensions—which we have as ideas—are part of this sensory world's inner structure. They are non-sensory.

The physical dimension, which enables objects and physical beings to have volume and to be juxtaposed in space, rises as a negation of these depths; it is born out of a lost relationship with the etheric and spiritual dimensions. These two dimensions, which can be grasped only abstractly, remain as the secret structure of the physical world. Because of their measurability, we always reduce them to the physical dimension without perceiving them.

A body's internal volume is always an image. We imagine this internal volume, but never see it. It is an ideal, invariable relationship that has something to do with a cube that can be enclosed within a fist, or one the size of the Himalayas. Its inner dimension is not subject to measurement.

True space is, therefore, the abolishment of the physical dimension—the negated inner depths. The negation itself becomes abolished. True space is not the entrance to a mythical fourth dimension. It is, rather, a discovery of space—the true earth. What we call the fourth dimension is inevitably conceived in accordance with a thought bound to three-dimensional space; it is conceived as a further projection of the sensory world subject to an identical expulsion from space.

Nevertheless, a difference exists between discovering (or reentering) space and never having lost it. For when we discover space, we carry there a force formed in the process of seeking space—of seeking it where it has become a mere shadow of itself.

Only the person who has cognized the will, which the physical Earth alone can arouse, possesses the capacity to move in space. This physical Earth stands in opposition to what moves it from the depths. Such an opposition can be removed only by the person who experiences it with the force of the will—a will stimulated by the Earth.

Therefore, it is not simply a matter of going "beyond" the space that we normally conceive; instead, it is a matter of reentering it. Of the three dimensions, the physical dimension needs to be eliminated. This does not mean losing the physical world but, rather, finding it within its true depths. These depths always escape human perception, feeling, and thinking until that final escape—death. The third dimension (or the dimension of death) conceals the secret of life.

– 50 –

Earth's etheric being is waiting for us to free it from its decrepit physical sheath; it is waiting to be liberated by the thinking that frees itself of sensory conditions.

In order for space to reawaken, we must overcome the third dimension where it mediates all reality, where it functions as the power of the physical organism that reflects thinking. In this way, space can reawaken as the space in which the spirit (as an "I") possesses its own movement all the way down to the mineral level. It does so without the mineral realm binding it to the law by which this mineral realm is itself presently governed.

The possibility of disenchanting the third (or physical) dimension does not mean losing the mineral world—which, currently, we can only perceive and abstractly think about—but, rather, rediscovering its profound structure and becoming articulated in it.

The third dimension, as a physical dimension, relates to the human being expelled from space who no longer possesses space, nor true breathing. It is the dimension of the depths, which we can experience as the creative power of space.

By removing the third dimension, we enter the invisible earth, where the life of minerals, plants, and living beings interweaves. To eliminate the third dimension is not to take something away or to lose the life element. Rather, it is to *discover* the foundations of life.

A plant's etheric being, like that of an animal or of a human being, is imprisoned within corporeality. It becomes active only within the mineral realm by being subjected to its metaphysical inertia.

Matter, either aggregated on the mineral level or permeated with life, constitutes the profound sleep of the etheric. Only by losing its power of presence in accordance with the spirit can this etheric furnish true space, or the inner dimensions of things. Such a possibility surfaces in human thinking.

We must discover the third dimension, which is the symbol of our expulsion from space.

The third dimension, however, cannot be discovered where we imagine the presence of physical space. Likewise, it cannot be discovered where we imagine the aggregations of physical matter—aggregations that depend on physical movements that do not manifest on their own, not even as nuclear energy. Nuclear energy unfolds only as the active power of the etheric forces' extra-spatial void, a power that governs the nuclear transmutations of substances and stands in opposition to them. Thus, we continually draw indirectly from a power that aggregates and disintegrates matter by way of matter itself—namely, from outside—without truly understanding the nature of our actions. This is precisely due to the fact that we base our knowledge on scientific experimentation and measurements that fail to grasp what lies behind the scenes of aroused phenomena.

Similarly, the corpuscular theory, the concept of coordinates and of a material point's quantities of motion, the concept of kinetic and potential energy related to a system of points, as well as wave-mechanics, all relate to the metric configuration of space, namely, to the physical space whose specter is all that we possess. Such a specter actually lives within us as an idea, but as one that we fail to experience.

$$- 51 -$$

It can therefore be said that it is *precisely* the physical dimension that is lost. Insofar as it is lost, the third dimension enchants thought, thereby enabling it to rise up. By moving from the physical dimension, thought is able to depict space metrically.

Thought possesses the secret of space within its movement. For the interweaving of its movement is the resurfacing of the fabric of original space, the form of our original inner world, of "lost paradise."

The human etheric body possesses this space as a form of universal spatial thought. By operating within the etheric's organism, such universal spatial thought always leads the etheric back to its own law.

Only human thought can utilize the etheric fabric that edifies our physical form to make the spirit's expression (or vehicle) independent of our etheric-physical corporeality. What expresses itself in the form of egoism in physical corporeality becomes the spirit's individual power when elevated to the etheric level by virtue of thought.

The etheric body is a magical model that keeps the original powers intact. Yet, it can also be an impediment to human freedom if thinking fails to disengage its etheric power from corporeality, or nature—which in turn can even appear mystical or ethical.

The true power of creative morality is the thinking that, by becoming the unforeseeable movement of the spirit, makes itself independent of each bodily and etheric process. Only this spirit movement has the power to resolve earthly evil.

The thinking that frees itself from the brain—the organ that enables it to reflect reality and render it dialectical—ceases to undergo bodily or psychic attachments. Such thinking has the capacity to actualize its innermost force, which alone can defeat earthly darkness and the heaviness of the soul.

This thinking has the power to penetrate the third dimension—the dimension of death—only if it can free itself from the etheric-physical body by activating its purest etheric forces via a movement that is itself free. It can create the spirit's individual vestment out of the etheric form.

By uniting with the physical being, individual form inevitably manifests as egoism. Transferred to the etheric body, this individual form expresses the spirit's individualizing power; it ceases to be egoism. Herein lies the ultimate meaning of egoism.

Earth's spatial-temporal sphere, namely, the sphere of darkness and death—for light is never seen, nor life ever had—is the field where the source of light within thinking can draw life forces from darkness and from death. These life forces enable us to experience what is living.

Space becomes lost whenever the creative forces of space within us are bound to corporeal being.

The spiritual space that the initiate turns to is not the etheric universe experienced after death. Rather, it is the earthly space that we redeem with the light forces of thought by impressing individual form—the vehicle of the spirit that becomes free— onto our etheric bodies.

Not only is this the secret of space but it is also the secret of individual thought as it stands out from universal thought; it is the secret of the human etheric body as it stands out from cosmic ether.

We will thus be able to move about in the space that we presently fail to see yet secretly yearn, in the space that we think we move in without ever reaching it truly at any given point.

We will be able to touch space. We will be able to cognize it, not as a universe into which we dissolve, but as a space of light where we will be able to perceive ourselves and move with our living being, corporeally articulated. This is all dependent upon a corporeality in which the spirit permeates the mineral element as it magically sculpts the etheric body, completing what thinking has always worked on—our individual form. This individual form is the mystery of humankind, the ultimate secret of thought's being.

The being of thought enables the etheric to become the spirit's vestment, thus bringing about its resurrection in that sphere of death known to us as the measurable world—that is, the sphere of the specter of space and time.

– 52 –

The space and time of rational human beings, the space and time of physics are nothing more than measures of a death process. Such space is never crossed; such time is never grasped. They are only the shadow-thought of the being of space and time, the shadow-thought of a reality to which they point and for which they manifest only to disappear into it.

Space and time have no other meaning. They are the measure of Earth's disintegrating sheath, of Earth's past that tends to remain current. They are the measure of what Earth has ceased to be, while an invisible earth rises like the germ of a new life from the sheath of the decomposing seed.

The forces that weave space surface within us as the form-forces of thinking, and as the form-forces of that 'imagining-thinking within perception' which enables the world's images to rise up with the power of reality. Though these images appear to linger before us by means of their own objective power, we already participate in their birth by means of those forces.

In forming the future Earth, such forces operate as the golden virtue of human thinking, feeling, and willing. From our inner life, they draw the golden movement that enables them to be the creators of a new cosmos. This can happen only to the degree that our inner life actualizes the secret of freedom and, thereby, frees itself from the enchantment of time and space, from the illusion that Earth's dying sheath is its reality.

By regarding *maya* as reality, by assuming ascetic or poetic attitudes that are opposite to spatial-temporal appearances, we fail to free ourselves of this illusion. These spatial-temporal appearances continue to manipulate us without us knowing it, for they manipulate us at the root of thinking. They take hold of thinking where it continues to live of its pure life, a life that nourishes the pure fabric of space-time.

The processes of space and time do not precede our perception and our thinking; they do not manifest apart from our breathing.

From the breath, we in fact receive the life forces that we recall and then lose in thinking and in perceiving.

In opposing these life forces, thought individualizes. To concentrate thought on the breath is to feed on the breath's life forces that have been killed.

Our breathing occurs within space and time devoid of life. Such life must be discovered within the profound forces of thought. Though we breathe by seizing the life needed by our corporeal being, we kill the light of this life in the process of consciousness. By estranging itself from life, this consciousness becomes self-consciousness.

Only when evil (or pain) continually takes away our breath are we able to draw directly from the *light* of the forces of life that ordinarily dies out in the breath. Only then are we able to free ourselves from the enchantment of space and from the enchantment of time. In reality, we free ourselves from them only at death.

But the practitioner of today must intuit that the death of the spatial-temporal illusion is inherently possible within the thinking that thinks about space, within the thinking that thinks about time.

– 53 –

The life of the original being of space and time has become lost. Therefore, by becoming ever-more bound to the sensory sphere, we human beings have called upon the breath to provide us with what impersonal thought has been unable to give us. Nonetheless, it *is* possible for the life of the original being of space and time to rise up again as thought's breath of light.

If the life of space and the presence of time are to rise up once again, thought must itself rise up; it must recognize its initial restoration of both the spatial and temporal wefts by expressing itself as a direct relation of the sense-bound multiplicity.

Such a relation does not come about in order to be deduced and translated into knowledge. Rather, it arises in order to be experienced as a world movement—as being. This demands that thinking draw from its most hidden forces, which are at one with the fundamental reality of such a relation.

If we fail to enliven the thinking that thinks about the world, then such thinking will not be able to draw from the world's life, notwithstanding the fact that it abstractly presupposes this life by drawing a lifeless science from it.

Thinking must pass from abstractness (its non-reality) to the manifestation of its own true being if it wishes to pass from mere sensory relations to the very reality that unites these relations—the suprasensory reality. Such a reality is not a mere abstract connection but, rather, life itself. In this way, it ceases to be discourse, argumentation, lifeless theory, or mechanical mediation but becomes, instead, the perception of the world's living element.

Cognition must be re-enlivened if it is not to be a mere incidental occurrence but, rather, the penetration of creation's architectural element, the penetration of that being which we fail to experience but which we conceive as space and as time.

In order for cognition to actualize its own power of life, it must experientially grasp its own process, which unfolds in the ordinary cognitive act. Such an act is aroused by sensory experience.

Thought must go from experiencing the world's objectivity to experiencing the *movement* that this objectivity arouses within us. Thus, the exercise related to the concentration of thinking must begin with a worldly object in order for thinking to grasp, within itself, the reality of its own being by setting aside the object's content, or meaning. This is the secret that enables thinking to actualize what it really is and ultimately to become the thinking that penetrates the world.

– 54 –

In order for the concentration of thinking to be the soul's living point of contact with the forces that weave space and time, it must be carried out according to the canon of the spirit that functions in the earthly realm, and *not* according to how it once traditionally operated. Only in this way will the concentration of thinking be true and lift the soul to the height of its breath where space-time is not merely its dead projection. Normally, however, we simply employ these weaving forces to think *about* space and time without possessing such thought.

By concentrating on an object, we do not limit thought. Instead, we employ the object—whose singularity stands before us as the symbol of all that belongs to the multiplicity—to evoke the unlimited force of thought. In its spatial-temporal alterity, such an object represents all the world's objects, which are not excluded from the world but, rather, virtually included in it.

Concentration reduces the multiplicity to a unity. It does not limit vision; instead, it enables us to evoke the forces of vision outside any spatial-temporal enchantment by utilizing a sign of that enchantment. These forces are evoked within a single point, which is the point through which we can reenter infinity.

The object that we need to re-evoke, without having it physically before us, is a symbol of the spatial-temporal world that again becomes thought—namely, the thought from which the object itself arose. This object must be simple and human-made in order to restore the thinking that once conceived it. Whereas we must contemplate the nature of minerals and plants through physical observation in order for nature to restore the living thinking concealed within it, such is not the case with a human-made object, if we observe well. It must, instead, be evoked in concentration without being simultaneously perceived, for it is only a manifestation of abstract human thought.

Thanks to concentration, the value of that particular objective form ceases to correspond to its conceptual meaning. Instead, its value lies in the presence of the formative force of representation, which, in effect, is the formative thinking force of any thought (or image) of sensory perception, possessed in its unequivocal, living movement.

Possessed in its living movement, this thinking force is the principle of the soul's revivification.

– 55 –

There are pseudo-ascetics or pseudo-masters with a following of disciples and worldly success, whose message, though dialectically plausible and comforting, does not demand work of any depth. Their teachings do not truly lead anywhere. These pseudo-ascetics (or pseudo-masters) present themselves as the bearers of a higher teaching by advising against concentration (among other things) as if they truly knew what concentration was, as if they truly understood its function at the present time.

Because concentration requires effort, these pseudo-ascetics (or pseudo-masters) insist that it binds, that it does not free. They insist that, by excluding other contents to the benefit of only one, concentration cannot possibly be the true gathering of forces.

It is evident that the limit of their thinking asserts itself in them as the incapacity to see the limit itself and, consequently, to exert the effort necessary for its elimination, among other things. This inner effort, however, *must* be exerted in order for thought to free itself from the intellectualism that binds it and thereby make it possible for us to arrive at that incorporeal communion with the spiritual realm, which is a profound willing that intensifies the more effortless it becomes. Our ultimate goal is to will effortlessly.

Furthermore, these pseudo-ascetics (or pseudo-masters) fail to see, within a theme of concentration, the content that thinking freely places before itself in order to exercise its dominion there. What they see, instead, is a content that conditions thinking, as if, from outside, this content had an autonomous force of its own. In this concentration theme, they fail to see the content, which, freed of its incidental form and discursiveness, becomes (at a given moment) the tangency with the world's inner content, thanks to concentration.

Concentrated thinking cannot sanctify the mutual exclusion of the world's objects, which is the illusory non-relation of physical space. But it can *overcome* such a mutual exclusion simply because all objects are similar with regards to their form and sensory reality. Therefore, a given object can symbolize any other. The simplest type of object is most useful in helping thought identify itself.

In truth, objects that mutually exclude one another exist only because of our inability to behold the thinking that once created them. Meanwhile, no serious researcher has ever doubted that spiritual contents can suffer the lack of relation appropriate to objects juxtaposed in physical space.

In order to manifest its pure force, free of the subtle permeations of feeling (and, therefore, of instinct), thinking must be devoted to a theme that can be objectively delimited without appealing to our inner life. Such thinking can then begin to actualize in the depths the spirit's profound disinterest and impersonality.

In reality, the rules for concentration and for meditation cannot just be given out by anyone incapable of grasping the process of thinking, that is, by anyone not officially sanctioned by the spiritual world itself. For personal wisdom is inevitably subject to egoic limits.

In this day, whoever objects to concentration—namely, to what is carried out according to the canon of thinking that actualizes its own movement within the sensory realm—is unfamiliar with the present-day spiritual path, regardless of the movement to which he or she belongs. Such a person cannot honestly orient anyone.

– 56 –

We can discover time. We can exist within time, as is never the case. In fact, we possess time as the thought of a passing that we measure only by utilizing the means of exterior space. We are not within this passing, nor do we live within it. We do not experience time by means of the inner forces that weave time, the life body, or memory body, which we can glimpse during a brush with death—our exit from time.

We can reenter the space from which we are separate and apart, from which we are exiled. Such space is imagined simply because we are outside it.

Our goal is to rediscover time and to reenter space; it is the goal of our lifelong journey.

Those of us who are schooled to perceive the thinking used to think about space and time, are aware of the attitude that begins introducing us to the secret of space and time—waiting.

Waiting is the inner exercise that draws from the living current of time.

Waiting is the calm within agitation; it is the patience that disenchants the imprint of exterior space-time within the soul.

The art of waiting calmly enables us to enter the mystery of ever-existing time; it allows us to enter a space that feels like the vestment of what we call eternity.

Eternity needs time in order to enter us; it needs time in order to accompany us to where we are confined (by the multiplicity) to a juxtaposition of things in space and to a succession of moments in time.

To reach a super-spatial and super-temporal point by means of contemplative concentration is not to escape time and space but, rather, to cognize the stream of forces that expresses itself within space and time. Freed of its spatial-temporal support, the soul is elevated to a relationship that enables it to experience, as simultaneity, the presence of the suprasensory realm from point to point, from moment to moment.

Therefore, concentration must be carried out long enough for pure time to subsist within the consciousness connected to the spatial-temporal dynamisms of the bodily support; in order for concentration to realize, within time, the timeless continuity of what is always present in its suprasensory form—which is time, discovered.

In concentration, we can realize the virtue of patience, just as in pure waiting we place ourselves opposite transitoriness. We are anchored in the calm perception of what has timeless value within measurable time.

In concentration, what we experience as the vestment of the spirit in its becoming (or punctual incompleteness) participates indirectly in what is already completed and followed up as completed—namely, the body that becomes and, in becoming, grows, is formed and ages. This support continually changes according to a spatial-temporal process that conditions the ordinary life of consciousness.

– 57 –

Life tends to rise up again in contemplation like a thought's breath of light, in which eternity's point of tangency with the transitory (that we can recognize in the rhythm of the universes, of the seasons, of day and night, of the breath, and of the beating heart) again becomes light's point of tangency with the life that normally dies out as thought, as icy dialectics, or as the life engaged in bodily processes.

This becoming proceeds from that rhythm. Nevertheless, it does so in order to extinguish it, in order to continually withdraw it from its sidereal power and make an earthly game out of it—a will *willed* in accordance with Earth. It is the light captured by corporeality, which meditation alone can restore. Through the power of meditation, we come to see that our bodily nature is secretly founded upon the light of thought, from which it can directly draw provided the meditation is profound.

If meditation is true—and such is rarely the case—our body ceases to be the isolator of the world, in opposition to abstract matter, for which matter is seen as something other, as something lifeless, as something bound to the space and time that are themselves dead.

The body discovers its own time. The soul discovers its own space, which, for corporeality, is time at that very point of becoming the rhythm maker of life. In reality, the secret is to enter the space that we imagine but fail to see.

– 58 –

Our misery and pain arise out of our separation from space. Entities exist outside us for we are incapable of entering their space. Because they exist outside us, we count them and weigh them; we systematize and render dialectical their impenetrability, or externality.

Our task is to enter space. We must not limit ourselves to measuring and mechanically overcoming dead space. The body that moves within such space can be enlivened by the rhythm of those forces that actually move it from the depths, so that we can cognize the space in which these forces move.

At the point in which we encounter the silence of the world's sounds and the exhaustion of each sound (including that of the highest music inevitably conditioned by earthly resonation), we can find an entrance to the space from which we have been expelled, just as we have been expelled from the life that we nevertheless intuit and feel pulsating within us and within the world.

We therefore reenter the original time that contains human history. Such history was, and will be, like a space in which we can truly move and communicate with the spatial weft of entities and events.

No other movement really exists. Our suffering arises because true movement—as well as true breath and true being— is impeded. We exist separate and apart from space, separate and apart from our breath. Each creative act, each undertaking, each rebellion, each human suffering is an obscure attempt to reenter space and discover the living stream of time. We exist

separate and apart from life, limited by the lifeless and measurable projections of space and time.

– 59 –

We have seen how the art of reentering space is a profound meditation. Such a meditation frees that being which is secretly at
one with the forces that weave the space and time of entities
illusorily foreign to us.

As a specter of what they really are, space and time began
to accompany humanity when human beings—with the light
of thinking lost—identified life with the light's extinct being.
Spectral projections of time and space arose as the lifeless reflection of the original light.

These spectral projections accompanied human beings as a
temporary support, as a sign that pointed to the thinking forget-
ful of its emanation from the secret light of the world.

Measurable space and measurable time point to what is dead
of the Earth—of the Earth that has ceased to exist. Earth's new
life presses forth within the light of thinking wherever thinking
avoids capture by the Earth's dying aspect. It presses forth like a
secret breath in which the human being is finally able to breathe.

In order for the world to be born at last, the measurable space
and time of the world must vanish. Though they will indeed one
day pass away, the principle of life (whose light is reflected in
space and time) will not.

This life principle is the germ of a future Earth, of an invisible earth, which already surfaces from the decrepit sheath
that human beings tend to sanctify as reality and elevate to the

height of culture and civilization. This life principle surfaces in the meditation of rare individuals. It surfaces in the thinking that frees itself from the earthly processes of death, from the specter of space and from the specter of time.

In truth, the art of reentering the secret of space and the secret of time is a profound meditation—as profound as the light of life from which it arises.

Counting
9 reunites the
multiplicity

The World (W)

7/8

the Secret Silence

Space/Time (S/T)

7/8 Conceived out of

A THINKING FABRIC

Movement

13/11 Supra Sensory

14 Thought

A Force

11

Machine

12

ZERO

12

CPSIA information can be obtained at www.ICGtesting.com
Printed in the USA
LVOW120238060613

337246LV00001B/4/P

9 781584 201304